Eating Sacred Cows

Also by Graeme Carlé and published by
Emmaus Road Publishing

Because of the Angels
Unveiling 1 Corinthians 11:2-16

The Red Heifer's Ashes
Mysteries of Ancient Israel

Born of the Spirit
A study guide for new believers

The Revelation series:
1. Dancing in the Dragon's Jaws
The Mystery of Israel's Survival

2. Slouching Towards Bethlehem
The Rise of the Antichrists

3. Gotta Serve Somebody
The Mystery of The Marks & 666

4. Silencing the Witnesses
Jerusalem & The Ascent of Secularism

Eating Sacred Cows

A Closer Look at Tithing

Graeme Carlé

Emmaus Road

*Dedicated to Dorothy Hayward & Yvonne Piper,
my wonderful friends whose prayers and widows' mites have sustained me!*

All proceeds from the sale of this book are used for the further publication of this and other similar work by Emmaus Road Publishing.

© 2015 Graeme Carlé
All rights reserved including the right of reproduction in whole or in part in any form. The moral rights of the author have been asserted.

First published as *Eating Sacred Cows (A New Look at Tithing)* 1988
Then as *Eating Sacred Cows (A Closer Look at Tithing)* 1994
Reprinted 1995, 2000
This revised, expanded edition 2015

Book design and production by Peter Aranyi
Cover by Olivia Carlé and Lorraine Bailey, AsOne Creative Design
Author photo by Ray Sheldrake

ISBN 978-0-9941058-1-3

International listing by Ingram Spark 2018

Unless otherwise stated, all Scripture quoted is from the NEW AMERICAN STANDARD BIBLE®, Copyright ©1995 The Lockman Foundation. Used with permission.

Emmaus Road Publishing
PO Box 38 823 Howick, Auckland 2014 New Zealand

Contents

Foreword to revised edition, 2015 1
Foreword to the 1988 edition 3
Introduction 5
   Extra-Biblical Sources – Jewish 6
   Extra-Biblical Sources – Gentile 8
1. The Old Testament 11
   Abraham's Tithe 11
   Jacob's Tithe 14
2. The Law of Moses 15
   "Whatever your heart desires" 15
   The Feast of Tabernacles, or Booths 17
   The Third Year 18
   The Differences 20
   Holiday Pay for the Tither 20
   Effect on the Levites 21
   Third Year Not A Simultaneous Cycle 23
   Effect on Widows, Orphans and Aliens 23
   First Fruits 25
3. The Prophets 27
   Amos's Rebuke 27
   Malachi and the Curse 27
   Nehemiah's Record 30
4. Revelation of the Character of God 31
   His goodness 31
   Our wholeness 32
   Confusion of the Old with the New Covenant 33
   "A Hard Man"? 35
5. The New Testament 37
   All Mentions of Tithing 37
   Conspicuous by Absence 40
   Jesus Himself 41
   The Twelve 42
   Paul & Co 43
   Robbing Churches? 46

6. Our Goal is An Attitude 47
One Rule Fits All? 47
Limited Resources 49
Tithing Unjust to Poor 50
Four Kinds of Lovers 52
Our Alabaster Vial? 54
7. A Punishing Tithe 55
Punishment for Teaching Tithing? 56
8. Lessons of the Old 59
Unrecognised Giving – Hospitality 59
Those Without Incomes 62
Widows and Orphans in New Testament Times ... 63
"Pure and Undefiled Religion" 65
The Poor in Our Time 65
The Ministers, In New Testament Times 67
The Ministers Now 69
9. Arguments for Tithing 71
1 Corinthians 16:1-2 71
"Tithing ensures giving" 72
"Tithing is a good start" 73
"I've been blessed for tithing" 74
10. Summary 75
11. How Then Should We Live and Give? 77
Karoshi, Death by Overwork 77
'No-Vacation Nation'? 79
Personal Testimony 81
Holidays In General 82
My Conclusions re Holidays 84
(i) Run and hide! 84
(ii) Three consecutive weeks 85
(iii) Mandated even by secular government 86
Personal Giving 87
Giving in general 89
The Poor 90
The Levites 90

    Our Experiments with Truth 92
    (i) No building 93
    (ii) No "blind" collections 94
    (iii) No central pool of funds 96
Last Word for Pastors **97**
    Without Fear 97
    With Perseverance 97
    Accurately 98
    Encouraging spiritual growth 98
    Faithfully building 98

Appendix A – Extra-Biblical Jewish References ... **101**
Appendix B – The Four Censuses of Israel **105**
    On leaving Egypt 105
    Forty years later 106
    David's muster 106
    Returning from exile 106
Appendix C – Israel's Holidays **109**
    Because of the Angels 112
    The Red Heifer's Ashes 112
    Born of the Spirit 113

Thanks

Many thanks to my friends and co-workers – for your love, encouragement, financial support, and sharpening – especially Arthur Amon, Peter Aranyi, Rory & Sarah Cavanagh, Chris & Melissa Hennessy, Mohan & Amy Herath, Kristin Herman, David & Louise Lee, Mike & Jill Meyer, Ben & Dolly Pan, Chris Pan, Shane & Melissa Pope, James Purves, Peter & Susan Ridley, Elizabeth Rowe, Ross & Jenny Shaw, Steve & Simone Varney, and, of course, Olivia.

*"And you shall eat in the presence of the Lord your God the
tithe of your grain, your new wine, your oil
and the first born of your herd and your flock
in order that you may learn to fear the Lord your God always"
— Deuteronomy 14:23*

Foreword to revised edition, 2015

I have long wanted to revise and update this book.

The 1988 original provoked strong reactions. I had naïvely assumed that everyone would be as delighted as I was at the revelation of God found in Deuteronomy 14, but unfortunately this was not the case. Some pastors in New Zealand denounced it from their pulpits; one preacher hurriedly dropped it without even reading it because he felt "there were demons on it"! Another actually burned it but the man who had loaned it to him then ordered 10 more so perhaps we should offer bulk discounts for book burnings!

More reassuringly, Dr Derek Prince read it and changed his stance, personally ordering 20 copies for his ministry's international council in 1989. He told them that they too should read it to prevent burn-out and his Canadian distributors ordered more.

As this became known, *Eating Sacred Cows* gained credibility; I was encouraged but also disappointed that so many Christians seemed unwilling or unable to read and trust the Scriptures for themselves. I am now more realistic. The Christian publishing market-place has so many competing publications, we often need a spur to consider any new or opposing perspective.

On the other hand, I have been delighted to hear many testimonies of a refreshing new freedom in those who have come to understand the new covenant more accurately through *Eating Sacred Cows*. Although now out of print, the original has been available for many years as a free download from websites in NZ, Korea, USA and Canada, which is gratifying. It has also been translated into French in South Africa. However, before reprinting, I wanted to strengthen my case by adding evidence from:

(i)   the Church Fathers

(ii) the example of Jesus, the Twelve, Paul and his companions

(iii) the widow's mite and Mary's alabaster vial

(iv) the consequences of our getting it wrong

(v) my own experiments with being more Biblical.

It is my hope and prayer that we will all prove to be true disciples of Jesus, abiding more carefully in His words so that we will know more of the truth which will set us free (John 8:31-32).

Graeme Carlé
December, 2015

Foreword to the 1988 edition

This study began as a much shorter discussion paper written in about 1981 to be considered amongst the leaders of the church to which I was committed for the eight years I lived in Christchurch. The church held tithing as a tenet of faith and we were asked to examine in turn all our church beliefs, so this was written to be discussed among friends and fellow workers. Since that time, the issue has come up many times in many places and the original study has been responded to, revised several times and circulated by photocopies, but I would like to improve the argument put forward - hence this publication.

I realise that in challenging the present general understanding of tithing that I am not just dealing with a doctrine but calling into question a major source of funding for church ministries and projects. This of course will cause some, especially those who are relying on consistent tithing, to want to avoid the discussion, fearing that people will stop giving if given half an excuse. If, however, what I'm saying is true and therefore the revealed will of God then we don't have to be anxious about provision because our heavenly Father knows our needs. What we should be concerned with then is surely not money but the will of God, knowing that if we get that right everything else, which includes how people give, will work out. This assurance of provision, as contained within Jesus' command to seek first His kingdom and His way of doing things, is just as surely for the leaders of churches and projects as for the people of those churches.

I sincerely make this case not to cause contention but because I believe truth will always be more liberating and fruitful than tradition and I would urge the reader to emulate the Berean Jews of whom it is testified:

> Now these were more noble-minded than those in Thessalonica, for they received the word with great eagerness, examining the Scriptures daily, to see whether these things were so (Acts 17:11)

If you find that I am wrong, in whole or in part, I want to assure you that I actively welcome further discussion and correction, and I would like to thank and acknowledge those who have already offered corrections and advice, especially David Lee for his constant encouragement and constructive criticism and the late Tom Marshall for his comments on my maths.

Introduction

I intend to show that there has been much misunderstanding of tithing, not only of what God requires of us today but even of what He used to require of Israel under the Law of Moses. Although some Christians do not tithe at all, most evangelical, charismatic and Pentecostal denominations teach that we should set aside 10% of all income we receive and give it to the Lord's work. Some believers in the older, more traditional, denominations give this to their church; others there give to "storehouses", defined as the more "alive" churches or ministries from which they receive most of their spiritual food. Some tithe on gross income (i.e. before tax or any other deductions) so that they are giving the Lord the first slice of the pie, while others tithe on their net income (i.e. after tax and/or other deductions) as they consider that is the amount they actually receive.

Which is the will of God? Is it perhaps an individual conscience issue with no single answer, so that we should take the Romans 14 approach of letting "each be fully convinced in his own mind"? I don't think so. I believe there is a single answer. I also want to counter undue coercion and legalism in the church of God and I'm sure there will be some surprise at the extent of it. For example, here in New Zealand I have come across the teaching of 30% tithing, the setting aside of three distinct tithes - one for the church or minister, the second to pay for conferences, and the third given away to the needy.

Even amongst respected Christian leaders, there is confusion over tithing. I was personally stirred to study it because I heard a very well-known Bible teacher, and one I greatly respect, Dr Derek Prince, state that he was afraid not to tithe because he believed he would receive a curse if he didn't. He based this on Malachi 3:8-9. He later changed his stance, as mentioned in the introduction, but we need to tread carefully because there are strong allies to whom we can look to confirm almost any view. The issue will only be properly resolved if we bother to dig a bit deeper – "seek and you *will* find".

Most importantly, we need to counter any misunderstanding because there is a revelation of the character of God in the Mosaic practice of tithing; any misunderstanding of that practice therefore means we miss out on that revelation.

Extra-Biblical Sources – Jewish

How have the Jews viewed tithing?

In the 3rd Century B.C., a light-hearted Jewish novella, *Tobit*, referred to two tithes, i.e. 20% per annum, but used in three ways:[1]

(i) one tithe was for the Levites

(ii) a second was for the poor and needy

(iii) every third year, the tither partook of the second tithe with the poor and needy, as a festal celebration.

In the 1st Century A.D., Josephus the Jewish historian wrote of three tithes:

> Besides those two tithes, which I have already said you are to pay every year, the one for the Levites, the other for the festivals, you are to bring every third year a third tithe to be distributed to those that want; to women also that are widows, and to children that are orphans.[2]

So he thought Israel's tithing was to be 20% for two years but 30% every third year.

In the 12th Century, Maimonides, also known as Rambam

---

[1] Full quotation in Appendix A.
[2] *Antiquities of the Jews,* Book IV, chap 8, sec 22, www.ccel.org/j/josephus/works/ant-4.htm, 24 Nov, 2013.

and "the second Moses", ruled on the basis of the Oral Tradition that it should be two, i.e. always 20%, for three purposes:

(i) the first tithe (*ma'aser ri'shan*) was for the Levites

(ii) the second (*ma'aser shani*) provided the festive feast for the tither and his family for two years but was given to the poor in the third year (*ma'aser ani*).[3]

Today, however, the authoritative *Encyclopaedia Judaica* disagrees, referring to two uses of one tithe (one for the Levites and one for a feast in Jerusalem) but carefully noting these were not simultaneous:

> The rabbis… interpreted them as two different tributes: one to be given to the levite, "the first tithe"; and the other to be brought to Jerusalem and consumed there, "the second tithe." Theoretically, this was an excellent solution. However, from the practical point of view the implementation of these laws was almost impossible. The excise of 20% of the yield was too high…[4]

In trying to discover present-day Jewish practice by discussion with our local rabbi, I found that the many different degrees of belief within Judaism result in many different practices of tithing. Some hold that since tithing was primarily an offering of the fruits of the land of promise, it can only be practised by those resident in Israel. Some friends of the rabbi in New York considered that feeding bread to the ducks at the park fulfils this part of the Law since it is the giving away of grain!

To summarise then, modern-day Jewish scholarship says the Law of Moses teaches tithing for three purposes but the outworking is left to individual conscience.

---

3 *Positive Commandments* 125-132, www.chabad.org/library/article_cdo/aid/901703/jewish/Part-2.htm, 25 Nov, 2013.

4 *Encyclopaedia Judaica*, ed. Michael Berenbaum and Fred Skolnik, 2nd ed., Vol. 19, Detroit: Macmillan Reference USA, 2007. Keter Publishing House Ltd, p. 739. Full quotation in Appendix A.

Extra-Biblical Sources – Gentile

In the 2nd Century, Irenaeus (A.D. 120-202) contrasted Jewish with Christian giving:

> And for this reason did the Lord, instead of that [commandment], "Thou shalt not commit adultery," forbid even concupiscence; and instead of that which runs thus, "Thou shalt not kill," He prohibited anger; and instead of the law enjoining the giving of *tithes*, [He told us] to share all our possessions with the poor…[5]

And again:

> And for this reason they [the Jews] had indeed the *tithes* of their goods consecrated to Him, but those who have received the liberty set aside all their possessions for the Lord's purposes, bestowing joyfully and freely not the less valuable portions of their property, since they have the hope of better things [hereafter]; as that poor widow acted who cast all her living into the treasury of God.[6]

Similarly, in about 197 A.D., Tertullian described how Christians were giving:

> Though we have our treasure-chest, it is not made up of purchase-money, as of a religion that has its price. On the monthly day, if he likes, each puts in a small donation; but only if it be his pleasure, and only if he be able: for there is no compulsion; all is voluntary.[7]

There is no doubt, as these two well-regarded Church Fathers testified, 2nd Century Christians were explicitly and deliberately not tithing but giving freely. Likewise in the 3rd Century - the *Didascalia Apostolorum* (circa 230 A.D.) explicitly ruled out tithing for Christians:

---

5 *Against Heresies*, Book IV, Chap XIII, Para 3. www.ccel.org/ccel/schaff/anf01.ix.vi.xiv.html, 10 Feb, 2015. Emphasis added.
6 *Ibid.*, chap XVIII, para 2. Emphasis added.
7 *Apology*, Chap XXXIX, Para 5. www.tertullian.org/anf/anf03/anf03-05.htm#P425_201743, 10 Feb, 2015.

> The Lord, by the gift of His grace, has set you loose and given you rest...that you should no more be bound with sacrifices and oblations, and with sin offerings, and purifications, and vows, and gifts, and holocausts,[8] and burnt offerings, and [Sabbath] idlings, and shewbread, and the observing of purifications; nor yet with *tithes* and firstfruits, and part-offerings, and gifts and oblations - for it was laid upon them [Jews] to give all these things as of necessity, but you are not bound by these things...[9]

Encyclopaedia Americana summarises:

> [Tithing] was not practised in the early Christian church but gradually became common [in the Roman Catholic Church in western Europe] by the 6th Century. The Council of Tours in 567 and the 2nd Council of Macon in 585 advocated tithing. Made obligatory by civil law in the Carolingian empire in 765 and in England in the 10th Century... The Reformation did not abolish tithing and the practice was continued in the Roman Catholic Church and in Protestant countries ... [until it was] gradually replaced by other forms of taxation. The Roman Catholic Church still prescribes tithes in countries where they are sanctioned by law, and some Protestant bodies consider tithes obligatory.

The Church of Jesus Christ of Latter Day Saints, or Mormons as they are usually known, which claims to be the restored early church and was formed in the latter part of the 19th Century, also considers the tithe obligatory.

---

8 It's easy to misread "holocaust" today because of the Holocaust in the 20th Century but this is a transliteration of the Greek word used in the Septuagint of the Hebrew name for the whole burnt offering (e.g. Lev 1:3).
9 *Didascalia Apostolorum*, IX, ii. 35, translated by R. Hugh Connolly, Oxford; Clarendon Press, 1929. www.earlychristianwritings.com/text/didascalia.html, 25 Nov, 2013. Emphasis added.

As for Eastern Orthodoxy, *Encyclopaedia Britannica* points out:

> The eastern Orthodox churches never accepted the idea of tithes and Orthodox church members have never paid them.

To summarise then, the Roman Catholic Church advocated tithing as long ago as the 6th Century while the eastern Orthodox churches, with similar antiquity, never accepted the idea. The Reformation maintained the Catholic practice unchanged and Protestant, Pentecostal and Charismatic churches today have differing views, some believing that all must tithe and some that it is up to each individual to decide.

Accordingly, as is usually the case, there can be no resolution of the issue if we only look at church practice or extra-Biblical sources. We must look carefully in the Scriptures to resolve it to our personal satisfaction.

1. The Old Testament

In this study, I use the terms Old and New Testament to describe two parts of our Christian Bible but Old and New Covenant to refer to the specific covenants made through Moses, i.e. the Law, and Jesus, i.e. "the new and living way" (Hebrews 10:19-20).

Abraham's Tithe

The first mention of tithing is in Genesis when Abraham, returning home with the spoils of a battle, met Melchizedek, the priest-king of Salem:

> And he [Abraham] gave him [Melchizedek] a tenth of all (Gen 14:20)

Why did he give a tenth? Why not a twelfth? Or an eighth? No explanation is given here but obviously because he was inspired to do so (Heb 7:1 ff.). In ancient Jewish thinking, ten was not only a number but it also had the metaphorical meaning of "all"[10] so a tenth was to symbolise that it all belonged to God and was due to His goodness. As Paul puts it:

> What do you have that you did not receive? And if you did receive it, why do you boast as if you had not received it? (1 Cor 4:7)

However, in considering today what Abraham did, we may come up against a major obstacle, a teaching that for many has obscured the whole issue. From this incident it is often taught that:

    (i)   Abraham predated Moses by some four hundred years so tithing was established before the Law and therefore apart from it.

---

[10] Details in my *Slouching Towards Bethlehem (The Rise of the Antichrists)*, pp. 36-39.

(ii) Christians are not under the Law of Moses but are still to follow Abraham's example in tithing.[11]

There are two serious flaws in this approach.

Firstly, those who teach this principle have to ignore other practices of Abraham which were just as surely established before the Law and yet are not for Christians.

What, for example, of circumcision "in the flesh of your foreskin" (Gen 17:11)? This was clearly the most important practice of Abraham, being the primary condition of the Abrahamic covenant (Gen 17:9-14), established before and apart from the Law, yet do those teaching tithing also advocate physical circumcision? In the Early Church, some of the Pharisees certainly did (Acts 15:1-5) and Paul had to strongly withstand them (Gal 5:1-12).

And what of animal sacrifices? Abraham offered animal sacrifices before and apart from the Law (Gen 12:8, 22:13). Do these teachers today advocate we offer these? Of course not, and I would agree with them (Heb 10:1-10). Then there is the issue of Abraham's concubines (Gen 25:6)...

So while the first proposition, that tithing predates the Law, is true and valid, the second, that Christians must tithe because of this, is false. In all sixty six New Testament references to Abraham, the only practice of his we are told to follow is having faith (e.g. Rom 4:11, 4:16; Gal 3:6-10). Some may still argue that we can infer a requirement to tithe from Hebrews 7:8, and we will look at that passage carefully later, but the point remains, there are no more New Testament commandments to tithe based on Abraham's example than there are to be physically circumcised, to offer animals as sacrifices, or to take concubines.

The second serious flaw in this approach to Abraham's

---

11 e.g. http://creflodollarministries.org/BibleStudy/StudyNotes.aspx?id=888, 16 Mar, 2015. This ministry has recently been in the news as raising funds to buy a USD $65m Gulfstream jet.

tithe is that Genesis does not explicitly tell us the purpose of the tithe, nor its frequency. As far as we know, Abraham only did it the once, from the spoils of a battle, and Melchizedek blessed him on that occasion. In Hebrews 7:1-8, where we are given the divine commentary on the significance of this meeting, there is no mention of it being a regular occurrence; the inference is that it only happened once. Basing the practice of tithing on this incident then, we should give away one tenth of a particular increase in our wealth and then stop!

As to the purpose of the tithe, we can safely infer it was in response to Melchizedek's ministry as a priest, when he brought out bread and wine for Abraham and blessed him. Hebrews 7 confirms this, telling us that the tithe proved that Melchizedek's priesthood is superior to that of Abraham's son, Levi. However, since even the newest Christian believer belongs to "the royal priesthood" (1 Pet 2:9), being in Christ who is our "high priest according to the order of Melchizedek" (Heb 5:10), every Christian should therefore be receiving tithes instead of paying them! Those teaching that we all need to follow Abraham's example of tithing surely need to explain why we are not all to follow Melchizedek's example of receiving them.

Actually Abraham was offering "first-fruits", which as we will see later was given primarily to the priests, and he chose a tenth of his recent gain to show his thankfulness to God. Unfortunately, this complicates the issue because under the Law of Moses, which is the only place we are given any explanation of these things, first-fruit offerings and tithes were different. They were given to different groups of people at different times and for different reasons. There is therefore much room for misunderstanding in this whole area so let's leave Abraham and "first-fruits" for now and see what the Scriptures do teach us plainly about tithing.

Jacob's Tithe

After Abraham, the second mention of this practice in the Old Testament is where his grandson, Jacob, vowed to God:

> "...of all that You give me I will surely give a tenth to You" (Gen 28:22)

At least here we can find evidence for a system of tithing rather than a one-off event. Again it appears to be voluntary, a thanksgiving offering since Jacob's vow is conditional on God's helping him (vss. 20-21) but again, there are no details as to how Jacob gave it. He may have offered it directly to God as a burnt offering, given it to one of God's servants like Melchizedek, given it in the name of the Lord to the poor, or disposed of it in some other way but we have no way of knowing what Jacob did.

2. The Law of Moses

It was not until the Law, four hundred years later, that tithing became mandatory or a general requirement for the people of God and it is only in the Law that the use of the tithe is actually explained. If we want to understand tithing, therefore, we have no choice but to study the Law, and here we will find another major flaw in our teaching today.

"Whatever your heart desires"

The main purpose of the tithe was not to support the Levites, as is usually thought today, but to provide the Israelites themselves with the feast for the Feast of Tabernacles. In modern terminology, the tithe was holiday pay!

For two out of every three years the tithe was not to be given away but was eaten by the tither and his household in the keeping of the Feast, to be enjoyed in the presence of God (Deut 14:22-26).[12] It was only in the third year the tithe was given away (Deut 14:27-29, 26:12). As we come to look at these Scriptures, we will see that modern Jewish scholarship is right in its application: although only one tithe was taken, it was used for two distinct purposes, as the *Encyclopaedia Judaica* says.

We see in Deuteronomy 12 that the tithes were to be brought to Jerusalem to be eaten by the tither, and shared with others:

---

12   The Feast of Tabernacles was celebrated initially at Shiloh (Jud 21:19) then primarily in Jerusalem but also in every city in Israel (Neh 8:15-16). We find this in Nehemiah's record of the restoration of Jerusalem, when "the city was large and spacious, but the people in it were few and the houses were not built" (Neh 7:4) because they were living "in all their cities" (Neh 8:15). They "made booths for themselves, *each on his roof*, and in their courts and in the courts of the house of God, and in the squares" (Neh 8:16).

> 17. "You are not allowed to eat within your gates *the tithe* of your grain or new wine or oil, or the firstborn of your herd or flock, or any of your votive offerings which you vow, or your freewill offerings, or the contribution of your hand.
> 18. "But *you shall eat them* before the LORD your God in the place which the LORD your God will choose, you and your son and daughter, and your male and female servants, and the Levite who is within your gates; and you shall rejoice before the LORD your God in all your undertakings." (Deut 12:17-18, emphasis added)

This is repeated in Deuteronomy 14:

> 22. "You shall surely *tithe* all the produce from what you sow, which comes out of the field every year.
> 23. "*You shall eat* in the presence of the LORD your God, at the place where He chooses to establish His name, *the tithe* of your grain, your new wine, your oil..." (Deut 14:22-23, emphasis added)

"The place where He chooses" was initially at the tabernacle of Moses in Shiloh (Josh 18:1, 1 Sam 1:3) but five hundred years later, when David captured Jerusalem, that became the "city of our God" (Psa 48:1), with the Temple where He established His name.

However, if the tither lived too far away from Shiloh or Jerusalem to carry his tithe there, he was to sell it:

> 25. then you shall exchange it for money, and bind the money in your hand and go to the place which the LORD your God chooses.
> 26. "You may spend the money for *whatever your heart desires*: for oxen, or sheep, or wine, or strong drink, or *whatever your heart desires*; and there *you shall eat* in the presence of the LORD your God and rejoice, you and your household." (Deut 14:25-26, emphasis added)

Notice, this feast was for the tither's "household", which included the children and servants, as in Deuteronomy 12:18

above, but was also extended to the local Levites, widows, orphans and strangers, as we will see next.

The Feast of Tabernacles, or Booths

For this week-long annual festival (Lev 23:39-43), Israel's families were to leave the security of their homes, travel to Jerusalem, and live in temporary shelters (tabernacles or booths) there, made of "the foliage of beautiful trees, palm branches and boughs of leafy trees and willows of the brook" (vs. 40). This was to be a vivid reminder to all succeeding generations "that I had the sons of Israel live in booths when I brought them out from the land of Egypt" (vs. 43). It was, if you like, a camping holiday.

It was also their harvest feast, being also known as the Feast of the Ingathering (Ex 23:16 and 34:22) and kept in the seventh month, "at the end of the [agricultural] year, when you gather in the fruit of your labours from the field" (Ex 23:16). Deuteronomy 16 describes its primary purpose as rejoicing:

> 14. "and you shall rejoice in your feast, you and your son and your daughter and your male and female servants and the Levite and the stranger and the orphan and the widow who are in your towns [i.e. your neighbours].
> 15. Seven days you shall celebrate... [in Jerusalem], because the Lord your God will bless you in all your produce and in all the work of your hands, so that you shall be altogether joyful" (Deut 16:14-15)

In other words, the first use of the tithe was to celebrate the goodness of God. The year's hard work was over - now they could relax and enjoy the fruits of their labours and God's provision, satisfying the legitimate desires of their hearts "in the presence of the Lord". No-one was to be left looking on as an outsider - they were to include any neighbours who had no harvest, including strangers or "aliens", e.g. refugees such as Ruth from Moab (Ruth 1:6-7).

This was in stark contrast to the fertility rites and festivals of greed, immorality, and drunkenness celebrated by the surrounding nations of the time, as well as by the preceding Canaanite peoples (Lev 18:24).

The Third Year

Now consider the second use of the same tithe. Deuteronomy 14 goes on:

> 27. "Also you shall not neglect the Levite who is in your town, for he has no portion or inheritance among you.
> 28. "At the end of *every third year* you shall bring out *all the tithe* of your produce *in that year,* and shall deposit it in your town.
> 29. "The Levite, because he has no portion or inheritance among you, and the alien, the orphan and the widow who are in your town, shall come and eat and be satisfied, in order that the LORD your God may bless you in all the work of your hand which you do." (Deut 14:27-29, emphasis added)

So we see that "every third year" the Levite, along with "the alien, the orphan and the widow", received "all the tithe", i.e. the whole tithe, not in Jerusalem at the Feast, but in the towns where they were living (vs. 28). This is repeated and explained further in Deuteronomy 26:

> 12. "When you have finished tithing all the tithe of your increase in *the third year, the year of tithing*, then you shall give it to the Levite, to the stranger, to the orphan and to the widow that they may eat in your towns and be satisfied.
> 13. And you shall say before the Lord your God, 'I have removed the sacred portion from my house, and also have given it to the Levite and the alien, the orphan and the widow, according to all Your commandments which You have commanded me' " (Deut 26:12-13, emphasis added)

Notice, the third year is called "the year of tithing" (vs. 12) because this was the only year the whole tithe was given away. In vs. 13, it is called "the sacred portion", i.e. it was the Lord's. The significance of this portion must not be underrated – it actually provided the physical means by which God would provide for those who looked to Him for their physical sustenance: the Levite, the stranger, the orphan and the widow.

Firstly, the Levites. In not giving the Levites any portion or inheritance of the land, God had promised them:

> "I am your portion and your inheritance among the sons of Israel" (Num 18:20)

He needed to give them an income, since He had taken away their ability to earn one, so He provided for the Levites in the third year tithe. We will consider how that worked out soon.

As for the stranger, the orphan, and the widow, this tithe was how God provided financial as well as moral support:

> The Lord protects the stranger; He supports the fatherless and the widow (Ps 146:9)

The Levites, strangers (or aliens or refugees), widows and orphans all partook of the "sacred portion", the portion of the Lord.

Some may object, "But what about that verse where the Lord says "to the sons of Levi... I have given *all the tithe* in Israel for an inheritance" (Num 18:21). Doesn't that mean the Levites received all tithes?" No, because Numbers 18 goes on to describe the tithe given to the Levites as "the tithe of the sons of Israel, which *they offer as an offering* to the Lord" (Num 18:24), or in other words, "the sacred portion". This description only fits the third year tithe as we have just read in Deuteronomy 26:13, "I have removed the sacred portion from my house, and also have given it..."

As for the tither and his family in the third year, the text does not give details so I assume that having given away the tithe, they celebrated the Feast from other 90% of their harvest, either up in Jerusalem or "each on his roof" (Neh 8:16).

The Differences

Summarising the two uses of the tithe, in normal years (i.e. the first two) the tithe was:

(i) taken to Jerusalem

(ii) eaten by the tither and his household and shared with those with nothing

(iii) an abundant provision to celebrate the harvest festival, the Feast of Ingathering, during which they left their homes to live in temporary shelters, so it was also called the Feast of Tabernacles or Booths.

In the third year, "the year of tithing", the tithe was:

(i) deposited in the nearest village, town or city

(ii) given in its entirety to those without an inheritance

(iii) to be the recipients' daily sustenance at home.

This plainly shows that even under the Law, tithing was *not* the automatic giving away of one tenth of all income and that the support of the Levites and others was actually the secondary purpose. When it came to the eating of sacred cows, as in this book's title, and the rest of the tithes, God gave all of Israel a portion and they each needed to know which was for them and which was not, lest they took someone else's.

So what was the outcome?

Holiday Pay for the Tither

The primary purpose of the tithe was to provide holiday pay, abundant holiday fare for the Israelites, showing that God has a wonderfully generous attitude towards His people. We still receive this in New Zealand, due to our civil law: all employees used to receive three weeks (now four weeks) annual leave plus two weeks of statutory holidays: two days at Christmas, two at New Year, two at Easter, one for Waitangi Day, Anzac Day, the Anniversary Day for each province, Queen's Birthday, and Labour Day. So the norm in New Zealand was five (now six) weeks holiday per year, i.e. from 9.6% to 11.5%, during which *we are paid to not work.* We receive that in our hands to spend during our holidays, surely a close equivalent to Israel's 10%, so that every time we go on our "secular" holidays we are actually enjoying the benefit of the tithe!

How ironic it is that while our secular government is behaving according to the Scriptures for the benefit of all, our churches have often instead turned it into a tax for themselves.

We will soon examine why God created this holiday provision but first let's consider the other major effects of the tithe not being given away for two out of three years, firstly on the Levites and then on the widows, orphans, and aliens.

Effect on the Levites

The obvious question is, would the Levites have received enough if they had only received the third year tithe?

The answer is yes. In fact, if they had received the tithe every year, they would have received *three times the annual income of everyone else!* We tend to think that since Levi was one of twelve variously sized tribes in Israel, the Levites must have made up about a tenth of the nation, so everyone else tithing to them would have created a fair portion for all. However, the size of the tribes varied significantly and the Levites were only ever about *one thirtieth* of the nation at most.

Consider Israel's first census. After the Exodus, they needed to organise their fighting men and they found that all the men of Israel over the age of twenty numbered 603,550

(Num 1:46-47, 2:32-33). The Levites, however, were counted separately from a month old and they numbered 22,000 (Num 3:39) which is one twenty-seventh of the population. And why would one month old Levite baby boys need tithes? Their Levite fathers would provide for their households. Accordingly, if 10% of the Levite males were under twenty, the ratio of over twenty Levites to over twenty Israelite male would be 1:30; if 20%, the ration would be 1:34.[13] If every other Israelite household had given every Levite household a tithe every year, the Levites would have received much more than their fair share.

The conclusion is unavoidable: it is only if the Levites received a tithe every *third year* that they would have received a fair and equitable portion with the rest of the nation.

We must not underestimate the importance of this equity, as have some who can't see a problem with the Levites getting three times the average income. The Scriptures specifically state that the giving of God's people..:

> ...is not for the ease of others and for your affliction, but by way of equality (2 Cor 8:13)

The Levites were supposed to receive *equally*, not to be at ease with more than enough while the givers were *afflicted* with less. A friend of mine, arguing for the Levites receiving a triple portion, referred to the eldest son being given a double portion of a father's inheritance (Deut 21:17) and the Levites being considered the first-born of Israel (Num 3:40-41). However, he was then unable to explain why the Levites were to receive a triple portion instead of the double. He was also overlooking the reason for the double portion of the first-born, that he was to provide for his mother at his father's death[14] rather than simply having more for himself.

---

13 Details of all four censuses of Israel are in Appendix B.
14 Jesus, being the eldest son, therefore ensured His widowed mother would be looked after when He died. (John 19:26-27)

Lastly, as can be seen in Appendix B, the population ratio must have been less than 1:30, and the Levite's portion therefore larger. This not only allowed for the widows, orphans, and aliens to have some of that tithe too (and we will consider their situation soon), but also allowed for the Levites to give away their "tithe of the tithe" to the priests (Num 18:26-28), without losing "equality".

Third Year Not A Simultaneous Cycle

The Levites receiving the third year tithe does not mean that they all received no income for two years and then all three years' supply in the third year. The third year seems to have been worked out on an individual basis, much like our present-day seven year retaining period of tax records, rather than a simultaneous cycle entered by all of Israel. I say "seems" because the Scriptures are not explicit and I have yet to find a reliable historical record of how this third year was outworked.

As I see it, every family's land was in the same Sabbatical or seven-year cycle but, because individual Israelites would normally have come into their inheritances at the death of their fathers in different years, they would be giving tithes in different years. This would also mean the Feast of Tabernacles could be celebrated in Jerusalem every year and not just for two years out of three.

Effect on Widows, Orphans and Aliens

Tithes never were the main income of widows, orphans and aliens/strangers/refugees; tithes were an extra so that they too had times of abundance. God had two other ways of providing for them, the first as a temporary measure and the other as a permanent solution. The first temporary measure was the gleanings of every harvest. God commanded His people:

"Now when you reap the harvest of your land, you shall

not reap to the very corners of your field, neither shall you gather the gleanings of your harvest. Nor shall you glean your vineyard, nor shall you gather the fallen fruit of your vineyard; you shall leave them for the needy and for the stranger. I am the LORD your God"
(Lev 19:9-10. Also Deut 24:19-22)

We can see from the book of Ruth how Naomi as a widow encouraged her Moabite daughter-in-law Ruth, who was a widow and an alien, to glean as the Law prescribed (Ruth 2:2, 2:23). There was ample temporary provision for the needy there. We can also see from the Book of Ruth the Lord's permanent solution: the kinsman-redeemer. Naomi knew of that and therefore encouraged Ruth to marry Boaz (Ruth 3:1-2, 9 and 13). Rather than supplying just material goods to meet needs, the Law helped establish relationships; instead of leaving the widow as a widow and the orphan as an orphan, always needing charity, God provided a way for them to be reincorporated back into a household. As Psalm 68:5-6 says:

> A father of the fatherless and a judge for the widows... God makes a home for the lonely [or as the *KJV* puts it, God setteth the solitary in families]

There was also the Sabbath year provision for the needy in Israel. God commanded all the farmers:

> 10. "You shall sow your land for six years and gather in its yield,
> 11. but on the seventh year you shall let it rest and lie fallow, *so that the needy of your people may eat*; and whatever they leave the beast of the field may eat. You are to do the same with your vineyard and your olive grove." (Ex 23:10-11, emphasis added)

It's worth noting that both the annual gleanings and the Sabbath year harvest were to be gathered by the needy themselves, granting them the same dignity of working for their income as everyone else.

First Fruits

In concluding this section on the Law of Moses, we need to briefly consider the offering of first-fruits; it is sometimes confused with the tithe because of the similarity of what was offered and because they are several times mentioned together (e.g. 2 Chron 31:4-6, Neh 10:35-39). Also, as mentioned earlier, Abraham's tithe to Melchizedek was the first-fruits of the spoils of a battle (Gen 14:20), which creates some overlap. Tithes and first-fruits were nevertheless distinct, being given to different groups of people at different times and for different reasons.

Israel as a nation was to celebrate the first-fruits of barley two days after Passover (Lev 23:14) and of wheat on the Day of Pentecost (Num 28:26). Every household was to set apart for God the first-born of every womb, both of man and beast (Ex 13:2, 12), the first products of every harvest of "grain, new wine, oil, honey, and of all the produce of the field" (2 Chron 31:5) and the first shearing of the sheep (Deut 18:4). In other words, first-fruits, first-born, first product and first fleece were given and consumed throughout the harvest, from the first month to the seventh; tithes celebrated all of the harvest from the third month to the seventh (2 Chron 31:7).

As to who received them, the high priest ate the two loaves of bread at Pentecost (Lev 23:20) while the rest of the first-fruits were eaten by the priests (Num 18:12-15, Deut 18:3-40). This is why Abraham gave his first-fruits of "the choicest spoils" (Heb 7:4) to Melchizedek the priest-king of Salem and did not partake of those with him - the fact that it was a tenth or tithe did not change its purpose. The Law's tithes, however, were eaten by the tither and his household, the Levites and the needy. The priests only received a tithe of the Levites' tithe (Lev 18:26-28).

In summary, first-fruits:
    (i)   Celebrated the beginning of the harvest.

(ii) They were consumed by the priests.

Tithing, however:

(i) Celebrated the fullness and end of harvest.

(ii) They were consumed in the first and second years by the tithers' household in Jerusalem at the Feast of Tabernacles.

(iii) In the third year, they were given to those Levites who were not priests and to the needy.

For 1,500 years, Israel's first-fruits festivals served as spectacular prophetic dramas, perfectly fulfilled on their exact days in 30 A.D. by the resurrection of Jesus and the outpouring of the Holy Spirit. Accordingly, the New Testament uses first-fruits as a metaphor for Jesus (1 Cor 15:20, 23) and the Holy Spirit (Rom 8:23). The first converts in an area were also described as first-fruits of the harvest there (1 Cor 16:15) and of 1st Century believers in general (Jas 1:18). These first-fruits predict that the harvest of earth was beginning then, the end of the harvest being the resurrection of all on Judgment Day (Rev 14:14-20).

In the meantime, the principle of acknowledging God as the source of every material blessing is seen in our giving of thanks for our meals. Praying in the name of Jesus devotes the food to God as we share it (cf. Rev 3:20) as priests with our "great high priest":

> God has created [all foods] to be gratefully shared in by those who believe and know the truth. For everything created by God is good, and nothing is to be rejected, if it is received with gratitude; for it is sanctified by means of the word of God and prayer (1 Tim 4:3-5)

The principle of first-fruits is also to be seen in our giving (Prov 3:9, 1 Cor 16:2), so we will look at this concept later.

3. The Prophets

Amos's Rebuke

Tithing is only mentioned twice in the prophets, once in Amos and once in Malachi, and on both of these occasions we find confirmation that the tithe was only given away in the third year. Indeed it is not until we have understood this that we can properly understand Amos's rebuke:

> "Enter Bethel and transgress;
> In Gilgal multiply transgression!
> Bring your sacrifices every morning,
> *Your tithes every three days...*
> For so you love to do, you sons of Israel"
> Declares the LORD God (Amos 4:4-5, emphasis added)

Bethel and Gilgal were the centres of idolatrous worship in the northern kingdom and Israel's fervour for the false gods was such that the Lord enjoins them ironically to give their "tithes every three days", instead of every three years.[15]

Malachi and the Curse

We now come to the last but most frequently quoted passage on tithing in the Old Testament:

> 8. "Will a man rob God? Yet you are robbing Me! But you say, 'How have we robbed You?' In tithes and offerings.
> 9. "You are cursed with a curse, for you are robbing Me, the whole nation of you!

---
15 Some translations have Amos 4:4 as "every three years" rather than the *NASB*'s "three days" because the Hebrew *yom* can have a number of meanings, just our English "day" does. It can mean daylight (Gen 1:5), a 24 hour period (Gen 1:8), time itself (Gen 4:3), a year (Ex 13:10) or an unspecified length of time, as in "the Day of the Lord" (Joel 2:11).

10. "Bring the whole tithe into the storehouse, so that there may be food in My house, and test Me now in this," says the Lord of hosts, "if I will not open for you the windows of heaven, and pour out for you a blessing until it overflows.
11. "Then I will rebuke the devourer for you, so that it may not destroy the fruits of the ground...
12. "All nations will call you blessed..." (Mal 3:8-12)

What is almost always taught from this passage is that God still requires every believer to give away one tenth of all income (in addition to all other contributions, donations and gifts) and that He will abundantly bless those who do and curse those who don't.

Before we look at the most emotive part of this teaching and whether this curse still operates under the New Covenant, let us examine the claim that the "whole tithe" mentioned here means "one tenth of all income" is to be given away, usually to the church.

As must be obvious from the earlier part of this study, not even under the Old Covenant did God make this general requirement that a tenth of all income be given away. Ironically, this passage from Malachi actually only further confirms the two different uses of the tithe since the tithe referred to here could only be the third year tithe.

Notice the specific points Malachi raised:

(i) Israel had "robbed God" by withholding tithes and offerings from His house, the temple in Jerusalem.

(ii) As a consequence, "the windows of heaven" were closed to them.

(iii) "A curse" was on the people and on "the fruits of the ground".

(iv) Israel needed to respond by bringing "the whole tithe".

(v) It was to come to "the storehouse" of the temple in Jerusalem.

If we now compare these with Deuteronomy 26:12-15, we find a perfect match as well as the curse explained. Take Malachi's first three points and then look at Deuteronomy 26 where the Israelites were to give away *the third year tithe*. They were commanded to pray:

(i) "I have removed the sacred portion from my house, and also have given it" (Deut 26:13)

(ii) "Look down from Your holy habitation, from heaven" (Deut 26:15)

(iii) "Bless Your people Israel, and the ground which You have given us" (Deut 26:15).

Malachi was similarly specific. It was the Israelites' failure to give that tithe that led to the conditions they faced. Because they had "robbed God" of the sacred portion, "the windows of heaven" were closed so God wasn't looking down with favour on them; instead of the Deuteronomic blessing they were to claim, they were left with the absence of blessing, i.e. a curse, both on the people and on the ground.

Now look at Malachi's last two issues:

(iv) Malachi refers to the "whole tithe". According to Deut 14 and 26, only the third year tithe was wholly given away; in the other two years, the tither's feast was shared with the Levites and the needy.

(v) The tithe was to be brought "into the storehouse, so that there may be food in My house". The only tithe that was to reach the temple in Jerusalem was either for the Levites who lived there or the tithe the Levites brought for the priests.

The parallels are inescapable – we simply cannot properly understand Malachi 3 without Deuteronomy 26.

Nehemiah's Record

We can see in Nehemiah 10 how this tithe got to the storehouse in Jerusalem when he records Israel's covenanted response to his and Malachi's urgings:

> 37. "We will bring... the tithe of our ground to the Levites, for the Levites are they who receive tithes in all the rural towns...
> 38. ...and the Levites shall bring up the tenth of the tithes to the house of our God, to the chambers of the storehouse.
> 39. For the sons of Israel and the sons of Levi shall bring the contribution of the grain, the new wine and the oil to the chambers" (Neh 10:37-39)

So the tithes that reached "the chambers of the storehouse" were for the Levites, i.e. the third year tithe, and the Levites' tithe of that tithe was to be given to the priests (Num 18:26-28) in Jerusalem.

4. Revelation of the Character of God

It must be abundantly clear by now that there is quite a difference between tithing as it is taught at present and tithing as God instituted it. Beyond all doubt, tithing was much more than a means of raising support for the Levites - it was an abundant annual provision for God's people to enjoy a holiday after the hard slog of harvest. But there's more yet. Deuteronomy 14:23 says the tithe was actually:

> "...in order that you may learn to fear the Lord your God always"

In other words, the practice of tithing was to further teach Israel why God should always be revered; in some way His character would be revealed and that would motivate them to serve Him. It was to be *a revelation of the goodness of God and His concern for their wholeness.* This revelation can still be sought today in a similar way.

His goodness

Not only does God want to be the origin of, and reason for, all our works (Eph 2:10, Col 3:17), but He also wants us to appreciate that He is the origin of all our holidays and rest-times. Our Government and our employers are merely, usually unwittingly, following His dictates.

For me this was a joy to find: God is interested in more than my faith, more than my works; He's interested in all of me, including my holidays and pleasures. I had tended to think of God as reluctantly conceding me time off so that I would be rested and refreshed in order to resume my work for His Kingdom. I now see there is no reluctance in Him but rather an earnest desire for me to have pleasure in my annual holiday. He is a generous and loving master and that certainly makes me love Him and want to serve Him more. Tithing in this way enables us to better *know Him*.

Our wholeness

The kind of holiday reveals God's concern for our wholeness. On their holiday, He specifically commanded Israel that they were to have whatever their hearts desired, to be enjoyed in His presence (Deut 14:26). This is still true today: our holidays are to be a time when the righteous desires of our hearts are satisfied. God knows that anyone living a life of self-denial, as every Christian should (Luke 14:26-27), can wander off His narrow way into the swamps of asceticism and the negation of individual personality. If we can never express our individual taste or preference, we become de-personalised.

I know from my own experience that if I have no opportunity to fulfil my heart's desire, I lose touch with my own heart. After a while I don't know any more what I actually do or don't like because I have been so busy working on what I should or shouldn't like! Hence, I believe, God's allowance for human frailty in the tithe for Israel and His means to ensure that we are fully rounded beings and *know ourselves*.

Irenaeus wrote in the 2nd Century:

> The glory of God is a man fully alive and the life of man consists in beholding God.[16]

This, of course, echoes Jesus' stated intention:

> "The thief comes only to steal and kill and destroy; I came that they may have life, and have it abundantly" (John 10:10)

This principle of sometimes allowing the heart's desires for

---

16 *Against Heresies,* Book IV, Chap 20, para 7.

righteous pleasures that are at other times to be denied also applies to *our knowing of others*. Let me give an example. For some time I worked in a very intensive way with a man called Jim whom I greatly respected but didn't know very well. We would go to an area where for months we would speak and teach, counsel and pray for folk. I well remember that on a two week visit to one place, we had about 50 meetings and appointments and it left us feeling quite burnt out.

After a while, we found that by insisting on a day off every week, usually Monday, we were actually more effective on the other six. And it was on that seventh day that I began to know more of Jim. On the days that we worked together, I saw and came to greatly respect his dedication, his skills, his discipline to the task and his self-denial, but on our day off, when he could do whatever his heart desired, I finally got to see a hidden part of his personality: he wanted to check out the local fishing and he loved to soak in hot pools. I too love soaking in hot pools so we would find one and soak in it! We found a common enjoyment, which increased our friendship and fellowship, and I learned a lot more of Jim.

Returning then to Israel's tithing, they were to learn to always fear the Lord by the sheer enjoyment of His provision to them in a time of rest and recreation, after a year of the self-discipline and self-denial of work. Seeing afresh His goodness and His concern for their whole being, whether at work or at rest, they would be motivated to serve Him afresh.

Confusion of the Old with the New Covenant

Having now gained a better insight into the Law of Moses, should we now as Christians tithe in this way? We obviously don't have to go to Jerusalem for the Feast of Tabernacles every year, but do we have to go on our holidays for two years and every third year give away our holiday pay to support a full-time Christian worker? Well, we should if the Holy Spirit tells us to, but if He doesn't, we don't have to.

While it is true that tithing was mandatory for Israel under the Old Covenant, things changed dramatically under the New Covenant and we can easily miss some of the differences. As mentioned earlier, I was motivated to study tithing because I heard Dr Derek Prince say that he was afraid not to tithe because he didn't want to receive the curse. He later changed his position after reading the previous edition of this book, but, for a time, even this wonderful Bible teacher thought and taught that non-tithing will bring a curse.

Christians are not blessed or cursed on the basis of tithing or not! On the contrary, placing ourselves under the law, even the law of tithing, will bring us under a curse:

> For as many as are of the works of the Law are under a curse; for it is written, 'Cursed is every one who does not abide by all things written in the book of the Law to perform them' (Gal 3:10)

One tract published by New Zealand Baptists claims that tithing "ALWAYS brings great blessing" (emphasis in the original). This is particularly disturbing, and yet appears to have gone unchallenged, because it claims a direct, causal link between a work of the Law and the blessing of God to Christians. Yet Paul wrote:

> 2. This is the only thing I want to find out from you: did you receive the Spirit by works of the Law, or by hearing with faith?
> 3. Are you so foolish? Having begun by the Spirit, are you now being perfected by the flesh? (Gal 3:2-3)

How easily we can forget and have to answer him, "Yes we have been that foolish; we have thought we are blessed by works of the Law". This is no small matter. Like Paul, we *must*...:

> ...not nullify the grace of God, for if righteousness comes through the Law, then Christ died needlessly (Gal 2:21)

The consequences to our spiritual life can be devastating whenever we, even unwittingly, minimise the work of the cross:

> 4. You have been severed from Christ, you who are seeking to be justified by law; you have fallen from grace.
> 5. For we through the Spirit, by faith, are waiting for the hope of righteousness (Gal 5:4-5)

"A Hard Man"?

This in turn can badly affect how we see God, until we become like the unfaithful servant, accusing Him of being too hard on us:

> 24. "And the one also who had received the one talent came up and said, 'Master, I knew you to be a hard man, reaping where you did not sow and gathering where you scattered no seed.
> 25. 'And I was afraid, and went away and hid your talent in the ground...' " (Matt 25:24-25)

Over the years, I've heard from struggling business people and solo mothers who had tithed under compulsion from their church's teaching. Worried by feelings of unrelenting condemnation, they had been further harassed by doubts as to the goodness of God. After all, they were being told He would curse them, and therefore their families, if they didn't give their tithes to the church.

One friend, Dorothy, told me of her internal battle. Her husband's business was in dire straits and, unable to afford to buy her son some new socks for school, she had gone to her husband's sock drawer to recycle some of his. There she saw some bundles of cash, set aside as their tithe, and began asking herself how could this be fair when her son needed clothes? This set off a round of self-condemnation as she rebuked herself for even questioning. She was eventually set free as she came to understand the New Covenant.

We must never be confused as to which covenant applies to us. It's the New and not the Old.

Let's now examine the New Testament.

5. The New Testament

All Mentions of Tithing

In the New Testament, tithing is mentioned, appropriately enough, ten times in all. The first two mentions are almost identical. Matthew 23:23 records Jesus saying:

> "Woe to you, Scribes and Pharisees, hypocrites! For you tithe mint and dill and cummin, and have neglected the weightier provisions of the Law: justice and mercy and faithfulness; but these are the things you should have done without neglecting the others."

Luke 11:42 adds that they tithed "every kind of garden herb" but disregarded "the love of God". So although Jesus rebuked their neglect of justice, love, mercy and faithfulness, He did commend the careful tithing of the Pharisees, for they even tithed food flavouring!

The third mention is the statement of the Pharisee that he paid tithes of all he received (Luke 18:12).

At first glance, these three seem to endorse Christian tithing because Jesus *did* say: "These things you should have done without neglecting... the weightier provisions of the Law". But notice to whom He said this - those under "the provisions of *the Law*", as He Himself was. What else could He say? Until Jesus died on the cross, thereby bringing in the New Covenant, the Old Covenant was in full force. See for example in Luke 5:14, where Jesus commanded the newly healed leper to "make an offering for your cleansing, *just as Moses commanded*". Those who want Christians to tithe because Jesus encouraged the Pharisees to do so, do they also want Christians to offer animal sacrifices because Jesus commanded the leper to do so? If not, why not? This offering of lambs and birds by cleansed lepers is certainly not now necessary, but equally certainly was, until Jesus died on the cross. He said:

> 18. "Truly I say to you ...not the smallest letter or stroke shall pass away from the Law, until all is accomplished.
> 19. "Whoever then annuls one of the least of these commandments, and teaches others to do the same, shall be called least in the kingdom of heaven"
> (Matt 5:18-19)

So these passages, although they are recorded in what we call the New Testament, are not yet teaching the New Covenant bur rather are more carefully explaining the demands of the Old Covenant.

Let's be very clear about this. It wasn't until after Jesus had lived a life that perfectly satisfied all the demands of the Law, until He was on the brink of dying on the cross, that He was able to say, "It is finished/accomplished!" (John 19:30 and Psalm 22:31). Only then could the New Covenant, established with His blood, i.e. by His death, come into effect.

The other seven mentions of tithing in the New Testament are all in Hebrews 7:

> 1. For this Melchizedek, king of Salem, priest of the Most High God, who met Abraham as he was returning from the slaughter of the kings and blessed him,
> 2. to whom also Abraham apportioned *a tenth part* of all the spoils, was first of all, by the translation of his name, king of righteousness, and then also king of Salem, which is king of peace.
> 3. Without father, without mother, without genealogy, having neither beginning of days nor end of life, but made like the Son of God, he remains a priest perpetually.
> 4. Now observe how great this man was to whom Abraham, the patriarch, gave *a tenth* of the choicest spoils.
> 5. And those indeed of the sons of Levi who receive the priest's office have commandment in the Law to collect

a tenth from the people, that is, from their brethren, although these are descended from Abraham.
6. But the one whose genealogy is not traced from them collected *a tenth* from Abraham and blessed the one who had the promises.
7. But without any dispute the lesser is blessed by the greater.
8. In this case mortal men receive *tithes*, but in that case one receives them, of whom it is witnessed that he lives on.
9. And, so to speak, through Abraham even Levi, who received *tithes*, paid *tithes*,
10. for he was still in the loins of his father when Melchizedek met him (Heb 7:1-10, emphasis added)

The question is, are we here being taught that Christians must tithe? Not for a moment.

Look at the context. This chapter is demonstrating the superiority of the Melchizedek priesthood, to which Jesus belonged (Heb 6:20), over the Levitical priesthood. It does this by reminding the Hebrews of the time when Abraham, the father of all Israel, gave a tithe to Melchizedek. The writer points out that under the Law, the Levites receive tithes from the rest of Abraham's descendants (vs. 5), but while still "in the loins" of Abraham (vs. 10), the Levites paid tithes to Melchizedek. This is not telling us to tithe. It is telling us that Abraham once did and this proves the superiority of Jesus' Messianic priesthood over the Law's Levitical priesthood.

However, even the newest Christian believer belongs to this "royal priesthood" (1 Pet 2:9) because we are all in Christ who is the "high priest according to the order of Melchizedek" (Heb 5:10). Those teaching that we all need to follow Abraham's example of tithing also need to explain why we are not to follow Melchizedek's example of receiving them!

To summarise:
i) Tithing is mentioned ten times in the New Testament.
ii) Three times speak of the need of the Jews of that day to keep the Law because, by the will of God, they were still under the Law.
iii) The other seven times are in a passage describing an Old Testament incident of giving, the point of which is to establish the superiority of Christ's priesthood over Levi's. It says nothing about New Covenant giving.

Conspicuous by Absence

If we now look at the many passages that teach specifically about giving under the New Covenant and compare them with the Old Covenant, there are three outstanding features.

Firstly, nowhere is tithing even mentioned! It is surely significant that although tithing was carefully and plainly commanded under the Old Covenant, as we have already seen (Lev 27:30-33; Num 18:21-28; Deut 12:5-19, 14:22-29, 26:12-14; Neh 10:34-39), it is completely absent from every New Covenant teaching on giving! There are at least forty passages, referenced later under "Those Without Incomes" - in 2 Corinthians alone, chapters 8 and 9 contain more verses than all of the Old Testament passages put together. There is a lot of opportunity there for tithing to at least be mentioned!

Secondly, rebuke for non-payment. In the New Covenant, there is no rebuke for non-payment of tithes even though in the Old Covenant it was carefully and powerfully rebuked as we have already seen from Malachi, but consider too Nehemiah's reprimand:

> "I also discovered that the portions of the Levites had not been given them, so that the Levites and the singers who performed the service had gone away, each to his

own field. So I reprimanded the officials... All Judah then brought the tithe..." (Neh 13:10-11)

Thirdly, New Covenant behaviour. Not only is tithing absent from New Covenant teaching, but it is also completely absent from every description of how the Early Church gave, even though that is described plainly (Acts 2:45, 4:34-37, 5:1-11, 6:1-6, 20:33-35, 24:17). Surely if tithing is supposed to be the central means of funding the Lord's work, as is often taught nowadays, we can expect to find some mention of payment or non-payment in the early church, but there is none.

Jesus Himself

The perfect example of how the Lord's work should be funded is to be seen in how the Lord Himself was funded for the three and a half years He was ministering in Israel. We *know* He didn't receive tithes because He wasn't a Levite:

> For it is evident that our Lord was descended from Judah, a tribe with reference to which Moses spoke nothing concerning priests (Heb 7:14)

Instead, He worked as a carpenter until He was thirty (Mark 6:3) and when He left that work to begin His ministry, He received voluntary contributions from those who loved Him and His work:

> 1. Soon afterwards, He began going around from one city and village to another, proclaiming and preaching the kingdom of God. The twelve were with Him,
> 2. and also some women who had been healed of evil spirits and sicknesses: Mary who was called Magdalene...
> 3. and Joanna the wife of Chuza, Herod's steward, and Susanna, and *many others who were contributing to their support out of their private means* (Luke 8:1-3, emphasis added)

The Twelve

Of the Twelve travelling with Him, at least four were fishermen who became "fishers of men" (Matt 4:18-22) so they weren't tithe-receiving Levites. Matthew, also called Levi, had been a tax collector (Matt 9:9, Luke 5:27) so he could have been a Levite[17] but he left that work. So, whereas the Levites received the third year tithes to enable them to work in Jerusalem as temple servants (Num 18:6 and 21) and in their home towns as civil servants (1 Chron 26:29-30), Jesus and the twelve apostles did not.

When Jesus sent them out, He initially told them to leave behind their money belts, trusting instead that they would be supported by those to whom they spoke (Luke 10:4-8). However, just before He was crucified, He told them to take their own money from then on (Luke 22:35-36). They also had a common purse for common expenses, looked after by Judas (John 12:6, 13:29).

After the Day of Pentecost, they received generous support from the private means of the wealthy among them, as did many new believers who had stayed on in Jerusalem to learn from the Twelve:[18]

---

17 David expanded the work of the Levites from Tabernacle and Temple service to include civil administration (1 Chron 26:29-32).
18 Some assume this means these early Christians always had everything in common but not so. The Day of Pentecost was a one day festival which required all Jewish men to come to Jerusalem from wherever they lived (Ex 23:14-17), most leaving their wives and children at home because they were "Parthians and Medes and Elamites, and residents of Mesopotamia, Judea and Cappadocia, Pontus and Asia, Phrygia and Pamphylia, Egypt and the districts of Libya around Cyrene, and visitors from Rome, both Jews and proselytes, Cretans and Arabs" (Acts 2:10-12). Accordingly, before they all went home to share the good news with their families, they needed to "devote themselves to the apostles' teaching" (Acts 2:42) in a temporary community that needed feeding and accommodating from "house to house" (Acts 2:46).

> 32. And the congregation of those who believed were of one heart and soul; and not one of them claimed that anything belonging to him was his own, but all things were common property to them...
> 34. For there was not a needy person among them, for all who were owners of land or houses would sell them and bring the proceeds of the sales
> 35. and lay them at the apostles' feet, and they would be distributed to each as any had need (Acts 4:34-35)

This really was a loving and generous community.

Paul & Co

Paul likewise did not receive the Levites' tithes because he was from the tribe of Benjamin (Rom 11:1). Instead, while in Corinth, he was in part-time ministry, teaming up with Aquila and Priscilla:

> 3. and because he was of the same trade, he stayed with them and they were working, for by trade they were tent-makers.
> 4. And he was reasoning in the synagogue every Sabbath and trying to persuade Jews and Greeks.
> 5. But when Silas and Timothy came down from Macedonia, Paul began devoting himself completely to the word... (Acts 18:3-5)

In other words, Paul supported himself as a tent-maker (vs. 3) while ministering in the synagogue every Sabbath (vs. 4) but then went into full-time ministry (vs. 5). It seems Aquila and Priscilla, his "co-workers in Christ Jesus" (Rom 16:3-5), worked this way too.

In Ephesus, Paul reminded the elders:

> 33. "I have coveted no one's silver or gold or clothes.
> 34. "You yourselves know that these hands ministered to my own needs and to the men who were with me.
> 35. "In everything I showed you that by working hard in this manner you must help the weak and remember the

> words of the Lord Jesus, that He Himself said, 'It is more blessed to give than to receive.' " (Acts 20:33-35)

This way of working gave Paul incomparably more credibility than today's tele-evangelists who unashamedly broadcast their coveting of their listeners' "silver or gold".

He also reminded the Thessalonians of how he, Silas and Timothy had provided for themselves:

> 9. For you recall, brethren, our labour and hardship, how working night and day so as not to be a burden to any of you, we proclaimed to you the gospel of God (1 Thess 2:9, cf. 1 Thess 1:1)

This would suggest Paul made tents whenever he wasn't preaching, and he urged us to follow his example:

> 7. For you yourselves know how you ought to follow our example, because we did not act in an undisciplined manner among you,
> 8. nor did we eat anyone's bread without paying for it, but with labour and hardship we kept working night and day so that we would not be a burden to any of you (2 Thess 3:7-8)

This way of working has also enabled missionaries to work in nations where the gospel is forbidden. In 1998, I had the wonderful privilege of meeting Dr Christy Wilson, one of the founders of Tentmakers International. In 1951, he and his wife Betty eased around Afghanistan's ban on missionaries by teaching in the Government's schools. He became acting principal of a high school, gave private lessons to the Crown Prince, and conducted an English course for Afghan diplomats. He also became pastor of the Community Christian Church in Kabul in 1952.[19]

Of course, Paul didn't rule out ministers and apostles/missionaries being supported by the saints. He affirmed the

---

19 www.tentmakersinternational.info/Life%20Speaks/lifespeaks.asp, 12 May, 2015.

right of those doing so:

> 5. Do we not have a right to take along a believing wife, even as the rest of the apostles and the brothers of the Lord and Cephas?
> 6. Or do only Barnabas and I not have a right to refrain from working?
> 7. Who at any time serves as a soldier at his own expense? Who plants a vineyard and does not eat the fruit of it? Or who tends a flock and does not use the milk of the flock? (1 Cor 9:5-7)

However, he and Barnabas chose not to:

> 12. If others share the right over you, do we not more? Nevertheless, we did not use this right, but we endure all things so that we will cause no hindrance to the gospel of Christ (1 Cor 9:12)

This meant that Paul often was…:

> in labor and hardship… in hunger and thirst, often without food, in cold and exposure (2 Cor 11:27)

> I know how to get along with humble means, and I also know how to live in prosperity; in any and every circumstance I have learned the secret of being filled and going hungry, both of having abundance and suffering need (Phil 4:12)

Just as Nehemiah, faced with the needs of the Levites, simply rebuked the people for not tithing, so too could Paul have rebuked the Christians, if the New Covenant required it. Instead he encouraged every believer to give freely, concluding:

> Let each one do just as he purposed in his heart; not grudgingly or under compulsion; for God loves a cheerful giver (2 Cor 9:7)

As far as we know, the only apostle who might have received tithes was Barnabas because he *was* a Levite (Acts 4:36). However, we are never told he did and, given the animosity he faced as a follower of Jesus (Acts 13:50, 14:2), it seems very unlikely.

Robbing Churches?

I love Paul's hyperbole in describing how he worked in Corinth, distancing himself from false and greedy apostles who dominated and insisted on being paid by the Corinthians:

> 7. Or did I commit a sin in humbling myself..., because I preached the gospel of God to you without charge?
> 8. I robbed other churches by taking wages from them to serve you;
> 9. and when I was present with you and was in need, I was not a burden to anyone; for when the brethren came from Macedonia they fully supplied my need, and in everything I kept myself from being a burden to you, and will continue to do so.
> 10. As the truth of Christ is in me, this boasting of mine will not be stopped in the regions of Achaia (2 Cor 11:7-10)

He "robbed other churches", i.e. in Macedonia, by accepting "wages from them" while serving the Corinthians in Greece.

Of course, most missionaries today live this way, depending on financial support from their sending church or Christian friends to serve in another land. I've personally worked like this for years both overseas and within New Zealand, working as a volunteer with Chinese immigrants, in home groups and writing at home while friends in other cities have faithfully contributed to my support.

6. Our Goal is An Attitude

What the New Testament clearly teaches is giving with liberality and sharing; its goal is a generosity of heart, rather than the paying of a tax. John wrote that giving is the natural outcome and evidence of loving:

> But whoever has the world's goods, and beholds his brother in need and closes his heart against him, how does the love of God abide in him? Little children, let us not love with word or with tongue, but in deed and truth (1 John 3:17-18)

Consider Paul's stated objective as a minister and the major teacher of the new churches when he wrote to the Philippians commending them:

> ...even in Thessalonica you sent a gift more than once for my needs. Not that I seek the gift itself, but I seek for the fruit which increases to your account (Phil 4:16-17)

What Paul was seeking was "the fruit" of generosity, evidence that they were growing in Christ, becoming more like Him.

One Rule Fits All?

What's usually the problem at this point is that we as Christians are often looking for one rule that we all have to live by. One rule, such as giving a tenth, keeps things simple; it can be easily learned by asking someone in the church what the will of God is and then we don't have to look any further to know how we should be living. In other words, we don't need to have a personal relationship with God! Fortunately, God knows about this and seems to deliberately thwart our desire.

If we eagerly look for one Scriptural role-model as to how much we should be giving, we find Jacob, who as we noted before, vowed to God: "...of all that You give me I will surely give a tenth to You" (Gen 28:22). So that makes it clear: we should all give one tenth of all our income, that is, we should tithe as it is usually taught today...

However, as we read on, we find to our dismay that Zacchaeus, a rich man, not only made restitution but also gave away *half* of his possessions to the poor (Luke 19:1-10). Should we all then give away 50% of all we own? No, because we then find that God's requirement of the "certain ruler... who was extremely rich" was that he was to sell *all* of his possessions, and distribute the proceeds to the poor (Luke 18:18-25). Should we all therefore give away everything we have? Was Zacchaeus half-hearted and Jacob a real cheap-skate?

There can never be just one rule.

God isn't so much concerned with the amount as with the *attitude of heart* of the giver.

What He wanted to accomplish in the heart of Zacchaeus at that time was achieved by Zacchaeus giving away half his possessions; what He wanted to achieve in the heart of the rich young ruler would only have happened if he'd been willing to give away everything.

On the other hand, what if some overly zealous but actually irresponsible disciple wants to give away everything and then be supported by others? It may be that this one is not to give away anything for a while, but is instead to pay his bills and learn faithful, unspectacular, stewardship.

Actually I believe God may lead us to do *all* of these at different times in our lives.

The conclusion then, is that the only rule that can apply is *not a rule for how much* we should give for a spiritual lifestyle: we are to give and share or even withhold as God may direct us in each circumstance and the way in which we do this measures our true spirituality (Rom 8:14). Accordingly, we must each cultivate our own, personal, relationship with

Jesus, to learn to hear His voice and walk in the Spirit of God. Only to the degree that we are *listening to and abiding in Him* will our lives be fruitful and our giving effective (John 15:4). The decision of how much to give is not left to a system or based on coercion, but rather to the purposing of each individual believer in relation to the perceived need and as a loving response. Our perception of the need, however, can be based on misrepresentation, through hard-sell, panic, or outright confidence tricks, so I believe we need to be more careful than ever to listen to the Holy Spirit. We also need to consider any prompting in the light of the following New Testament Scriptures to be sure it is Him. We may be in for some more surprises!

Limited Resources

It is obvious that God has unlimited resources. Seeing this, we Christians can presume that we have too, but consider the parables Jesus told us of what He gives us to use. In Matthew 25:14-30, the man going on the journey gives five talents to one slave, two to another two, and one to another,[20] 'each according to his own ability' (vs. 15). The first two slaves then

---

20 We use 'talent' today to describe natural abilities, e.g. in talent quests, but in Biblical times, a talent was a unit of weight, being approx. 30 kgs or 66 lbs [www.jewishvirtuallibrary.org/jsource/History/weightsandmeasures.html, 21 Oct, 2015]. As a unit of money, usually in silver, it was worth about 6,000 denarii. Since one denarius was a standard day's wage for a labourer (Matt 20:2) and they worked six days a week, a talent was about 20 years' wages. The 'five talents' was therefore 100 years wages, the 'two talents' 40 years. In New Zealand today, with our average wage of $50,000 p.a. in 2014, a talent would be about NZ$1 million [www.stats.govt.nz, 24 Feb, 2015]. In the USA in 2014, with the average wage of about US$54,000 p.a. [www.deptofnumbers.com/income/us, 22 Oct, 2015] so one talent would be about US$1.1 million; in the UK, the average wage in 2014 was about 25,000 GBP p.a. [www.tradingeconomics.com/united-kingdom/wages, 22 Oct, 2015], making one talent about 500,000 GBP.

double the amount he gave them while the third refuses to act and hides the talent in the ground.

In Luke 19: 12-27, the nobleman going to receive a kingdom for himself gives his slaves a mina each with instructions to "do business with this" in his absence.[21] One slave makes ten more minas, another five, but again one slave refuses to use it and simply hides it.

In both parables, the master is disappointed and angry at the last slave's refusal to use what they were given. In neither does the master say "Never mind that you've wasted all your opportunities - here's some more," because by then it's too late.

While it's true these parables can apply to all of our abilities, we today can over-spiritualise them to exclude our finances. Let's apply them to our finances. Over our life-times, we simply do not have unlimited money. What we do with what we have is therefore very important to God – if we waste it on self-indulgence, we will be held accountable. If we appear selfless by giving it away but do so without thought or love (1 Cor 13:3), God is not impressed since He gains nothing from our irresponsibility. We should each aim to be a "good and faithful slave" of our Master.

Fortunately for us, we do not usually receive all of our income or gifts at once. Every time we receive something, we have a fresh opportunity to be a good and faithful slave. We should use our limited resources in the ways that God would have us use them and not waste our giving opportunities, even when tempted to within the church of God.

Tithing Unjust to Poor

It may seem that tithing is fair because it's the same for everyone. However, tithing is unjust to the poor and can actually cripple them. Remember how Jesus taught about the

---

21 A mina was 1/60 of a talent, i.e. 100 denarii or about four months' income, or NZ$16,700, US$18,300 or 8,300 GBP today.

huge difference between rich and poor?

> 41. And He sat down opposite the treasury, and began observing how the people were putting money into the treasury; and many rich people were putting in large sums.
> 42. A poor widow came and put in two small copper coins, which amount to a cent.
> 43. Calling His disciples to Him, He said to them, "Truly I say to you, this poor widow put in more than all the contributors to the treasury;
> 44. for they all put in out of their surplus, but she, out of her poverty, put in all she owned, all she had to live on." (Mark 12:41-44)

Today we describe this "surplus" (vs. 44) as discretionary spending: it's the amount that is left over after we've paid for the necessities of life, i.e. food, clothing and shelter. The rich can have a substantial surplus whereas the poor may have a shortfall and increasing debt, as many poor people who have tithed can attest today.

It isn't hard to see this and even our tax departments tax lower incomes at a lower rate but, sadly, many church leaders don't consider or check the effect of their message. They just keep preaching tithing as if it were fair.

Compare the very different situations of three income earners.

The first one earns our NZ average annual income of about $50,000, as above. Paying tax of about $8,500, their tithe of $5,000 would leave them a net income of $36,500. They don't have many luxuries and without additional work, many one-income families only just manage to live on that.

The second earns $200,000 annually. Their tax of about $60,000[22] and tithe of $20,000 still leaves them with $120,000,

---

22 First $14,000 at 11.95%, next $48,000 at 18.95%, next $70,000 at 31.45% and the last $130,000 at 34.45% (approx. figures only, not allowing for tax minimisation).

enabling them to enjoy more luxurious living and to give much more, as Jesus noted at the Temple treasury.

However, the third earns only $25,000. Taxed about $3,800[23], they now have $21,200, which may be less than their outgoings on rent, food and clothing for their family. What then should we make of them being taught to pay a tithe of $2,500 to their church? They are being asked to give, as Jesus said, "out of all they have to live on".

Urging the poor to tithe, with this disproportionate impact, is manifestly unjust.

Four Kinds of Lovers

How can we get a perspective on our own situation? Am *I* generous or am *I* selfish?

Many years ago, my friend Jim Doak drew my attention to four "lovers" in Paul's last letter:

> 1. But realize this, that in the last days difficult times will come
> 2. For men will be *lovers of self, lovers of money,* boastful, arrogant, revilers, disobedient to parents, ungrateful, unholy,
> 3. unloving, irreconcilable, malicious gossips, without self-control, brutal, haters of good,
> 4. treacherous, reckless, conceited, *lovers of pleasure* rather than *lovers of God*... (2 Tim 3:1-4, emphasis added)

We can be "lovers of self", "lovers of money" and/or "lovers of pleasure" rather than "lovers of God".

I see this as a very practical self-diagnostic tool for each of us. We can identify if we are truly lovers of God rather than selfish, greedy or hedonistic simply by considering *how* we spend our money. Of course, we are to take care of ourselves and, as already mentioned, that includes enjoying holidays.

---

23 First $14,000 at 11.95%, next $11,000 at 18.95%.

God wants us to prosper in all respects and to be in good health, just as our souls prosper (3 John 2).

However, after I've paid for the genuine necessities of my life - food, clothing and shelter - *how much of what's left* do I spend on myself and how much do I actually give to others?

In Western society today, while we don't openly worship idols as they did in Canaanite, Greek or Roman times, we do often unwittingly worship what Jesus called *Mamonas*, or Mammon (Matt 6:24), i.e. the personification of wealth. We may see it as materialism or consumerism and, of course, we would never bow down before a pile of money to worship it as the Creator. However, "worship" comes from the Old English concept of worth-ship. So, to what do we accord the most worth or ultimate value in our lives? The answer can usually be seen in how we spend our money. Is it for God and in His ways, or for ourselves and in our ways?

As I see it, this is a primary test of, and opportunity for, our personal spirituality:

> 6. But godliness actually is a means of great gain when accompanied by contentment.
> 7. For we have brought nothing into the world, so we cannot take anything out of it either.
> 8. If we have food and covering, with these we shall be content.
> 9. But those who want to get rich fall into temptation and a snare and many foolish and harmful desires which plunge men into ruin and destruction.
> 10. For the *love of money is a root of all sorts of evil,* and some by longing for it have wandered away from the faith and pierced themselves with many griefs.
> 11. But flee from these things, you man of God, and pursue righteousness, godliness, faith, love, perseverance and gentleness (1 Tim 6:6-11, emphasis added)

We can all practise being content with what we do have, "food and covering" (vs. 8), instead of "longing" for money (vs. 10) because of what we don't have. In this way, we are worshipping God and growing spiritually.

Our Alabaster Vial?

We can also negate our love of money by choosing to be generous or gifting it to the Lord.

Remember the woman and her very costly alabaster vial of perfume? It was worth over three hundred denarii (Mark 14:5) so, with a denarius being the equivalent of day's wages, it was virtually a year's wages she lavished on Him! Jesus reproved those criticising her:

> 6. ..."Let her alone; why do you bother her? She has done a good deed to Me.
> 7. "For you always have the poor with you, and whenever you wish you can do good to them; but you do not always have Me.
> 8. "She has done what she could..." (Mark 14:6-8)

Notice the Lord's comment about the poor – "whenever *we wish*, we can do good to them" – and we can also give large gifts. Luke adds another comment:

> "For this reason I say to you, her sins, which are many, have been forgiven, for she loved much; but he who is forgiven little, loves little" (Luke 7:47)

She loved much and gave much because she knew the depth of His forgiveness. If we want to love Him more and become more generous, we may need to take the time to consider exactly how much *we too* have been forgiven.

7. A Punishing Tithe

It is with some trepidation I raise this issue as I know it will be contentious and may be abused by some who hate the church of God. However, we who love the church must not avoid the issue because that only leaves room for our opponents, and we must walk in the light of all the Scriptures.

There was another tithe taken in Israel which we usually overlook. God expressly warned Israel about it and when they ignored His warning, He left them to suffer under it as a punishment. If we ignore His warning, we too will suffer under it.

In about 1050 B.C., God told Samuel to warn Israel of what would happen if they set up a king over themselves:

> "This will be the procedure of the king who will reign over you... He will take *a tenth* of your seed and of your vineyards... He will take *a tenth* of your flocks and you yourselves will become his servants" (1 Sam 8:11, 15 and 17, emphasis added)

This tithe was to provide the king with all the trappings of his power: the army, the palace, the land holdings, and the banquets, with a hierarchy of servants to look after everything.

> Nevertheless, the people refused to listen to the voice of Samuel, and they said, "No, but there shall be a king over us." (1 Sam 8:19)

It is not surprising then, human nature still being what it is, that from at least the 6th Century A.D., the state church of Rome set up its own kingly authority, imposed tithing, established armies, palaces, cathedrals, and lands, for the Pope, his princes, the cardinals and bishops.

In Israel, these trappings included the king's harem, Solomon's leading to his downfall (1 Kings 11:1-10). This too we have faithfully repeated throughout church history with recurring sexual immorality, especially throughout the Dark Ages.

Those of us who are Protestant and/or Pentecostal have no place for self-righteousness in that we too have repeated this mistake. It is surely no coincidence that those amongst us most promoting tithing often have building programmes in mind, hold strongly to hierarchical leadership, and are just as likely to fall into immorality. The very structure being promoted creates extra temptations, far more than God would have us face.

What am I saying then? That there is, and always has been, a tithe that God expressly warns us about, being called for by those repeating Israel's mistake. God allowed the mistake to be made then, and allows it today, as punishment for our disobedience to His gentle voice.

Part of our suffering will be a knowledge of lost opportunities to use to maximum effect the limited talents He has given us. If we have buried our talents and minas in unproductive church assets - our cities have many empty or under-utilised church buildings – those talents and minas were not available for the work of God and we will each have to give an account to our Master when He returns.

Punishment for Teaching Tithing?

As a minister myself, I often recall the parable Jesus gave every pastor, elder, preacher and teacher:

> 42. And the Lord said, "Who then is the faithful and sensible steward, whom his master will put in charge of his servants, to give them their rations at the proper time?
> 43. "Blessed is that slave whom his master finds so doing when he comes.
> 44. "Truly I say to you that he will put him in charge of all his possessions" (Luke 12:42-44)

We who minister the word of God are the stewards put "in charge of his servants, to give them their rations at the proper time". Every one of us who is "faithful and sensible" to do so will be rewarded.

> 45. "But if that slave says in his heart, 'My master will be a long time in coming,' and begins to beat the slaves, both men and women, and to eat and drink and get drunk;
> 46. the master of that slave will come on a day when he does not expect him and at an hour he does not know, and will cut him in pieces, and assign him a place with the unbelievers.
> 47. "And that slave who knew his master's will and did not get ready or act in accord with his will, will receive many lashes,
> 48. but the one who did not know it, and committed deeds worthy of a flogging, will receive but few. From everyone who has been given much, much will be required; and to whom they entrusted much, of him they will ask all the more" (Luke 12:45-48)

Let's be very clear about Jesus' severe warning here.

Every steward who is not "faithful and sensible" will be punished to varying degrees: the one who badly abuses the master's servants will be "cut in pieces" and cast out "with the unbelievers" (vss. 45-46); the one who knows but does not "act in accord with the master's will" will be severely punished (vs. 47) while the one who doesn't know it but acts badly will receive a lesser punishment (vs. 48).

What are these abuses?

The worst are "to beat" the people of God, which can be physical, sexual or spiritual abuse, and to take more than our share of our Master's goods, "to eat and drink and get drunk" (vs. 45). Obvious examples to me are cult leaders like

Moses David Berg,[24] Jim Jones,[25] David Koresh,[26] or Joseph Kibwetere.[27] These men will be held to account at the Lord's return.

Much less extreme are godly leaders who fail to "act in accord" with what they know of "his will" (vs. 47). They may lead churches who publicly shame those who do not tithe, disobeying Jesus' commands for us to not "let the left hand know what the right hand is doing, so that your giving is in secret (Matt 6:3-4). These leaders will "receive many lashes" when the Lord returns, i.e. they will not be lost but they will be severely punished, presumably by pangs of remorse and shame. Our churches' giving policies have too often caused stumbling and Jesus plainly warns us:

> "Woe to that man through whom the stumbling block comes!" (Matt 18:7)

Lastly, what of those who don't know the master's will but, even with good intentions, act badly?

As I see it, this includes those teaching tithing as an obligation when, as we've seen, it is not His will. We are all free to tithe but no one is obliged to tithe. James warns us:

> Let not many of you become teachers, my brethren, knowing that as such we will incur a stricter judgment (Jas 3:1)

Those of us who are teachers will be more strictly judged, both for what we teach and how we live it out. We *will* also be held to account for how we treat the rest of our Master's servants.

---

24   Between 1968 and 1994, Berg turned his Children of God into sexual playthings.
25   In 1978, at Jones's Peoples' Temple in Colombia, 914 drank poisoned Kool Aid or were shot.
26   In 1993, sexual predator Koresh led the Branch Davidians into a siege in which 86 died.
27   In 2000, Kibwetere's Ugandan Movement for the Restoration of the Ten Commandments of God caused the deaths of at least 924 men, women and children.

8. Lessons of the Old

How then should we use our money? Where should we give?

Although we are not under the Old Covenant law of tithing, we can still learn from it today, firstly in recognising God's provision and the benefits of holidays, as in two out of the three years, and secondly, by recalling where God wanted the third year tithe to go.

Although the New Covenant does not include tithing to determine *how much* we should give, its directions as to *where to give* are identical with the second use of the Old Covenant's tithe. In both covenants there is a consistent loving concern for those without an income: the poor (the widows, orphans, and strangers) and the Levites (ministers and missionaries, i.e. those called to leave other work for the sake of the work of God).

Before we look at the obvious, let us consider the not so obvious.

Unrecognised Giving – Hospitality

In one area of giving, there is no actual handing over of cash. I was initially surprised to find that in the 1st Century, the primary way of giving was hospitality. Of course, when I thought about it, it was obvious – opening up our homes for hospitality can be very costly in both financial and personal terms. This is especially so when we are providing accommodation and/or meals for people to whom we wouldn't normally relate, for whom we bear no first-hand responsibility, or wouldn't even know.

At the Resurrection, Jesus says some believers will be astonished at being called "the blessed of My Father" for, among other things, *inviting in strangers* (Matt 25:31-46). Strangers are by definition away from home and unknown and are thereby poor or needy, at least in emotional or social terms if not in financial. Many in the church today are already giving freely in this way but don't fully recognise that they are giving according to the will of God. Some even feel condemned that they aren't contributing much. I spent seven years as an itinerant evangelist in New Zealand and on many occasions, I received in this way from folk who, I believe, will be surprised at their reward on the last day.

Giving to strangers also specifically fits John's description of giving as the natural outcome of loving (1 John 3:16-18) since the Greek noun for hospitality is *philoxenia*, literally, love shown to strangers. To be hospitable is to be loving and all the saints are commanded to give in this way. Consider Hebrews 13:2:

> Do not neglect to show hospitality to strangers, for by this some have entertained angels[28] without knowing it.

In Romans 12:13 we are told to literally "pursue hospitality" and 1 Peter 4:9 urges us to "be hospitable to one another without grumbling". God knows it's not always easy!

John adds, in regard to itinerant preachers and teachers:

> 5. Beloved, you are acting faithfully in whatever you accomplish for the brethren, and especially when they are strangers;
> 6. and they have testified to your love before the church. You will do well to send them on their way in a manner worthy of God.
> 7. For they went out for the sake of the Name, accepting nothing from the Gentiles.
> 8. Therefore we ought to support such men, so that we may be fellow workers with the truth (3 John 1:5-8, cf. 2 John 10-11)

---

28 The Greek, *aggelos*, lit. messengers, can refer to either spirit beings (Matt 4:11) or humans (e.g. Luke 7:24 cf. Luke 7:19-20). Abraham and Lot entertained spirit beings in human form (Gen 18:2 cf. 19:1) whereas Rahab, human spies (Josh 2:1). See also the author's *Because of the Angels (Unveiling 1 Corinthians 11:2-16)*.

Moreover, hospitality to strangers is a mark of spiritual maturity: a qualification of an elder of the church is that he is to be "hospitable" (Grk, *philoxenos*, loving the strangers) (1 Tim 3:2, Titus 1:8), and the widow who is to be supported by the church should have shown her willingness to serve the Lord by good works, including "if she has shown hospitality to strangers" (1 Tim 5:10).

Jesus also commanded us:

> 12. ..."When you give a luncheon or a dinner, do not invite your friends or your brothers or your relatives or rich neighbours, otherwise they may also invite you in return, and that will be your repayment.
> 13. "But when you give a banquet, invite the poor, the crippled, the lame, the blind,
> 14. and you will be blessed, since they do not have the means to repay you; for you will be repaid at the resurrection of the righteous" (Luke 14:12-14)

Notice, the meal and hospitality is giving but if repaid in kind, it's no longer giving. In the time of Jesus, in the absence of the Welfare State, to be physically handicapped and unable to work meant you would have no income. While today in N.Z. our tax system ensures that all have a minimum income, and thus the desperate need disappears, the principle does not diminish. As noted above, our needs are more than just material needs which an income can satisfy; they are also social and emotional, and the giving of love and friendship as shown in hospitality to strangers, the poor, and the handicapped remains essential to their (and our) welfare.

We will look at the poor later, but who are our "strangers" and our "crippled, lame, and blind"? I believe our strangers are not only refugees and visitors from overseas but also those who differ from us in race, culture, abilities, age, and income. Our handicapped are not only those literally handicapped but any who are weak where we are strong, and we may be their handicapped where they are strong and we are weak:

> Now we who are strong ought to bear the weaknesses of those without strength and not just please ourselves (Rom 15:1)

Our giving here is to be motivated by a loving, inclusive concern for all of our neighbours, especially the widows, orphans and strangers, and those who are called to leave other work for the sake of the work of God, i.e. the missionaries and ministers.

Those Without Incomes

All New Testament passages that teach or describe giving direct it into only two places: the various needs of the poor and an income for the ministers.

The Poor
Matthew 5:42, 6:2-4, 19:21
Matthew 25:31-46, 26:6-13
Mark 10:21, 12:41-44, 14:3-9
Luke 6:30, 10:30-37, 14:12-14
Luke 16:9, 21:1-4
Acts 6:1-6, 20:33-35, 24:17
Romans 12:13; 15:26-28
1 Corinthians 13:3, 16:1-2
2 Corinthians 8:1-24; 9:1-15
Galatians 2:10
Ephesians 4:28
1 Timothy 6:17-19
Hebrews 13:16
James 2:15-16
1 John 3:17-18

The Ministers
Matthew 10:9-10, 41-42
Mark 9:41
Luke 8:3, 10:7
1 Corinthians 9:7-14
2 Corinthians 11:8-9
Galatians 6:6-10
Philippians 4:10-19
1 Timothy 5:17-18
3 John 5-8

Several passages (Acts 2:45, 4:34-37 and 5:1-11) are not specific to one of these two groups; both the needy and the ministers appear to be included. Romans 12:8 mentions no particular direction for the giving, simply encouraging liberality.

However, Romans 15:26-27 points out that we Gentiles partaking of the Jews' spiritual blessings owe them material blessings (Rom 15:26-27. See later reference to 1 Cor 16:1-2).

Widows and Orphans in New Testament Times

Just as in the Old Testament God made two special provisions for the relief of the poor, one temporary and the other permanent, so too in the New. The widows and orphans, having lost their main provider with the death of the husband or the parents, and in the absence of our present-day Welfare State,[29] were to be particularly aided by His people:

> This is pure and undefiled religion in the sight of our God and Father, to visit orphans and widows in their distress, and to keep oneself unstained by the world (Jas 1:27)

In fact, we see the emergence of a welfare society in the early church's first concerted actions in this regard:

> 1. Now at this time while the disciples were increasing in number, a complaint arose on the part of the Hellenistic Jews against the native Hebrews, because their widows were being overlooked in the daily serving of food.
> 2. So the twelve summoned the congregation of the disciples and said, "It is not desirable for us to neglect the word of God in order to serve tables.
> 3. "Therefore, brethren, select from among you seven men of good reputation, full of the Spirit and of wisdom, whom we may put in charge of this task…" (Acts 6:1-3)

Firstly, we see the care for the widows was shown in a "daily serving of food", not from tithes or gleanings but primarily from those who could afford to give:

---

[29] In New Zealand, our taxes pay for state-owned housing and superannuation for those over 65, as well as social security payments to solo parents, invalids, the sick and the unemployed, including refugees.

> ... for all who were owners of land or houses would sell them and bring the proceeds of the sales, and lay them at the apostles' feet; and they would be distributed to each as any had need (Acts 4:34-35)

That this was a voluntary generosity is evident from Peter's rebuke of Ananias' *pretence* of generosity, when he reminded Ananias:

> "...while [the land] remained unsold, did it not remain your own? And after it was sold, was it not under your control?" (Acts 5:4)

He and Sapphira were only judged by God for lying to Him (Acts 5:1-11).

Secondly, we see the apostles' understanding that they weren't to do everything as leaders; this task which needed men "full of the Spirit and of wisdom" was not to be under their charge since they were called to proclaim the word of God. Accordingly, they looked for others who were godly enough to properly care for the widows' needs.

Paul later wrote in 1 Timothy 5 regarding how to set the church in order:

> Honour widows who are widows indeed (1 Tim 5:3)

He then goes on to define who is a widow "indeed" and needing support from the church: she "who has been left alone", "without children or grandchildren". Children and grandchildren are to "first learn to practise piety in regard to their own family and to make some return to their parents" (vs. 4). He warns that "if anyone does not provide for his own, and especially those of his household, he has denied the faith, and is worse than an unbeliever" (vs. 8). Later he notes that relations who can assist should assist "and the church must not be burdened, so that it may assist those who are widows indeed" (vs. 16).

Then we find Paul looking for the permanent provision of

God, the "nearest kinsman" of Ruth to be the redeemer, when he adds that only widows over the age of sixty are to be "put on the list" (vs. 9) for permanent support, while the younger ones are to remarry (vs. 14).

Of course, this aid from the church was in addition to individuals giving as led by the Spirit of God.

"Pure and Undefiled Religion"

It's no coincidence true spirituality is seen not only in "keeping oneself unstained by the world" but also in such practical matters as visiting "orphans and widows in their distress" (Jas 1:27). Likewise in Acts 6:1-3, "the daily serving of the food" for the widows, was to be undertaken by seven who were "full of the Spirit and of wisdom". True spirituality is also seen in the family of the widow caring for her as well as in plain, ordinary hospitality, the inviting in or love of strangers.

Seen in this light, Mother Theresa can only be recognised as a wonderfully spiritual woman, even if we cannot agree with everything she said.[30]

The Poor in Our Time

I have no expertise in economics but here's how I see some of the issues here in New Zealand in 2015.

For almost a hundred years now, our Welfare State has funded the relief for those in need through National Superannuation, the Domestic Purposes Benefit, the Sickness Benefit, the Unemployment Benefit etc. and by means of high taxation (I say "high" because of a Biblical incident which can give us some perspective. In 1 Samuel 8:10-18, when God warned Israel of the

---

30   For example, "There is only one God and He is God to all; therefore it is important that everyone is seen as equal before God. I've always said we should help a Hindu become a better Hindu, a Muslim become a better Muslim, and a Catholic become a better Catholic." www.ewtn.com/motherteresa/words.htm, 27 Oct, 2015.

consequences of their desire for a human king, He told them that the future demands of the king would cause them to suffer such hardship that they would call out to Him for help, yet these demands included only a tenth of their means as a civil tax).

So, whereas the Israelites individually were to take care of the needy and pay a low tax, today in New Zealand, the State takes overall care of the needy in our society and therefore imposes a higher tax. This in turn has taken away much of the need for Christians to directly support the needy in New Zealand. However, as groups such as Christians Against Poverty (CAP)[31] demonstrate, there is still a huge need for advocacy, mentoring, and budgeting advice.

The main stumbling block for us is that, whereas ancient Israel had many commandments to every individual to love and look after the poor, and prophets to remind them if they didn't, in our society today individual greed is strongly encouraged and rewarded, the poor are often blamed, and individual spirituality is actively scorned by our secular leaders. It is therefore a relief to see in NZ that, with the lowering of welfare benefits, it is our churches leading the way in re-establishing food banks.

Overall, however, there is in our society provision for the poor, with Christians and non-Christians alike giving to that end through the payment of taxes. Our help for the poor should therefore primarily be going overseas to places lacking welfare systems. We see this in Paul's urging the churches in Greece and Macedonia (2 Cor 8:1-9:15) to respond to the predicted famine in Judea (Acts 11:28-30):

> 1. Now concerning the collection for the saints [in Jerusalem], as I directed the churches of Galatia, so do you also.
> 2. On the first day of every week each one of you is to put aside and save, as he may prosper, so that no

---

31 Christians Against Poverty, www.capnz.org

collections be made when I come.
3. When I arrive, whomever you may approve, I will send them with letters to carry your gift to Jerusalem (1 Cor 16:1-3)

We can do this today through Christian relief organisations such as International Needs,[32] Interserve,[33] Servants to Asia's Urban Poor,[34] TEAR Fund,[35] and World Vision,[36] staying abreast of developments as policies can change with any change of government.

The Ministers, In New Testament Times

In ancient Israel, the Levites and priests were called to leave all other employment, i.e. their means of obtaining an income, in order to serve God full-time. In the New Testament, we find an exact parallel in the ministers of the gospel. Paul wrote:

> Do you not know that those who perform sacred services [i.e. the Levites] eat the food of the temple, and those who attend regularly to the altar [i.e. the priests] have their share with the altar? So also the Lord directed those who proclaim the gospel *to get their living* from the gospel (1 Cor 9:13-14, emphasis added)

Not now confined to only the Jewish tribe of Levi, this calling was still for only a few rather than for all believers. The ministers[37] like Paul (Col 1:23) were to serve God in "full-time ministry" by proclaiming the gospel and teaching (Col 1:25-29, 1 Cor 9:6-7, 11-12) and this, of course, includes all missionaries. As we saw earlier, Jesus Himself left His work as a carpenter at

---

32 International Needs (NZ), www.internationalneeds.org.nz
33 Interserve (NZ), www.interserve.org.nz
34 Servants to Asia's Urban Poor, http://servantsasia.org
35 TEAR Fund (NZ), www.tearfund.org.nz
36 World Vision (NZ), www.worldvision.org.nz
37 From Latin, *minister*, a servant, this best translates the Greek, *diakonos,* which has often been Anglicised as "deacon", without any translation.

age thirty and called a few others to do likewise; Peter, Andrew, James, and John all left their fishing nets to become "fishers of men" (Matt 4:18-22), Matthew left his tax-gathering (Matt 10:3). Their financial support came from other believers:

> ...many others... were contributing to their support out of their private means (Luke 8:3)

John wrote of giving in this way to propagate the truth:

> 5. Beloved, you are acting faithfully in whatever you accomplish for the brethren, and especially when they are strangers;
> 6. and they have testified to your love before the church. You will do well to send them on their way in a manner worthy of God.
> 7. For they went out for the sake of the Name, accepting nothing from the Gentiles.
> 8. Therefore we ought to *support such men*, so that *we may be fellow workers with the truth*. (3 John 5-8, emphasis added)

Paul writes that those who hear the truth should respond: "...and let him who is taught the word share all good things with him who teaches", adding that such giving is "sowing to the Spirit" (Gal 6:6-10). He uses a similar metaphor in 1 Corinthians 9:11, asking "...if we sowed spiritual things in you, is it too much if we should reap material things in you?". The hearers were to give in response to what they had received from the person to whom they were giving. This was the way of the early church.

The Ministers Now

The biggest difference between then and now is that today most ministers and missionaries are allied with and work for a particular denomination or organisation, drawing wages from it, and the saints therefore no longer give directly to the individual but rather to the denomination or organisation.

This can work well where the organisation exists for the support of the workers. Unfortunately, most organisations develop a life of their own, as do most bureaucracies, and the funds, instead of supporting more and more workers, are diverted into more and more facilities, or maintaining and improving them for the organisation itself.

Because our denominations usually insist on their own buildings, in many cities and towns we often have many small groups of believers each rattling around in their own large building, and not fully realising the incredible waste of limited resources.

I once briefly worked with a man whose congregation was meeting in the youth hall because it wasn't worth heating the main church building for the small number coming. The hall was new but there were no youth and in his town there were several other small groups representing the other denominations also meeting in large buildings, so we talked about it. His sad reply was that although he wanted to work more with the other churches in town, his denominational headquarters wanted to keep their flag flying there so he had to maintain the facilities no matter what else happened, and the other groups were in the same situation. The youth hall had been built because of a bequest, not because of a need, the youth of the town already using nearby facilities!

Many ministers see this happening but don't know the way out of such a waste of facilities. While this is outside the scope of this study, I believe it can be tithing that keeps the whole silly business going. If you and I were more careful to give more specifically to supply the income of the ministers and missionaries rather than giving to corporate schemes, many foolish or wasteful building projects would never get started or maintained.

On the other hand, if we want to attend a church with expensive facilities, it is only reasonable we all pay our fair share of the running costs, as we do with any social or golf club. At this point, we are not "giving" anything – rather, we are paying our dues and we still need to consider how we should give. Conversely, some church buildings are highly utilised for community and medical services, counselling, youth etc., all of which are worthy of our support.

9. Arguments for Tithing

1 Corinthians 16:1-2

Some teach from this passage that Paul means tithing, so let's consider it:

> Now concerning the collection for the saints, as I directed the churches of Galatia, so do you also. On the first day of every week let each one of you put aside and save, as he may prosper, that no collections be made when I come.

It is said that in the change from the agrarian and rural culture of Israel, with its annual harvest, to the suburban living of the Corinthians with their weekly income, the Israelites' yearly tithe was simply replaced by the city dwellers' weekly tithe. But was it? What was this collection and for how long was it made?

Firstly, we see from the following verse that the collection was for the saints who lived in Jerusalem (1 Cor 16:3). It was added to the gifts from the brethren from Macedonia (2 Cor 8:1-4, 1 Cor 16:5), and Paul wrote that it was for the poor in particular:

> it pleased those from Macedonia and Archaia [inc. Corinth] to make a certain contribution *for the poor* among the saints who are in Jerusalem (Rom 15:26-27, emphasis added)

From an earlier but very similar collection taken up in Antioch (Acts 11:27-30), it seems that in times of famine the poor among the saints in Jerusalem were hit particularly hard, perhaps cut off from their families for following Jesus (Matt 10:34-37). City dwellers may also not have much land to cultivate.

Secondly, the collections were only for a time. Paul went on to say:

> At this present time your abundance being a supply for their want, that their abundance also may become a supply for your want - that there may be equality (2 Cor 8:14)

In this instance the collections were made for about a year (2 Cor 8:10 and 9:2).

So this wasn't Paul teaching tithing; it was a systematic collecting of gifts for about a year for a particular need, "the poor ...in Jerusalem", for that particular time. Implicit in this teaching is that if the Corinthians were ever in need, those in Jerusalem would respond to them.

This was a loving redistribution of wealth in response to another country's problem.

"Tithing ensures giving"

Some have told me, "What you're saying is excusing people to *not give*". However, what I'm saying is that we are being excused from the Law's tithing system. We are actually called to give not one tenth to God but *ten tenths*. Jesus said:

> Not one of you can be My disciple who does not give up all his own possessions (Luke 14:33)

We must first do this. We must actually hand over everything we have to Him – ourselves, our relationships, family and friends, our houses and cars, our tastes in art, music, and reading material, plus all of our income and savings.

Anything less is not enough.

Only then, after we have handed over all our possessions to Him personally, can we be properly under His instruction. If we truly want to be His disciples, we then have to learn to hear His voice as He exercises His authority over everything He has left in our stewardship:

> 31. So Jesus was saying to those Jews who had believed Him, "If you continue in My word, then you are truly disciples of Mine;
> 32. and you will know the truth, and the truth will make you free" (John 8:31-32)

This is part of the adventure of being a disciple. We must learn to give freely and as regularly as He directs, which means we sometimes give nothing at all but simply pay our debts; sometimes we give only the amount we can afford to give and sometimes we give more than we can afford, trusting Him to meet our needs. If at times in our learning we give too much, provided that others relying on us don't suffer, God doesn't mind – generosity is, after all, giving more than is necessary – but at all times our motive must be love for the Lord and each other.

The New Testament teaching is to love and share:

> 16. We know love by this, that He laid down His life for us; and we ought to lay down our lives for the brethren.
> 17. But whoever has the world's goods, and sees his brother in need and closes his heart against him, how does the love of God abide in him?
> 18. Little children, let us not love with word or with tongue, but in deed and truth (1 John 3:16-18)

"Tithing is a good start"

Some say, "This is all very well in theory but in practice people don't give enough, so tithing is a good starting point". Sometimes they add that the Law is a tutor to bring us to Christ (Gal 3:24). However, if we are incorrectly teaching the Law regarding tithing, how are we bringing people closer to Christ?

Even if we had the Law right, I would ask: rather than follow Moses and teach tithing, wouldn't it be better to follow Paul and teach individual responsibility? Did Paul not understand practice as well as theory? He wrote in Romans 8:3-5 that *the Law failed* because of human weakness but that the Spirit can help us in our weakness. If we should therefore encourage people to walk in the Spirit, can't He teach them to give properly?

Shouldn't we put more faith in the word and power of God than in the wisdom of men (1 Cor 2:5)?

"I've been blessed for tithing"

Christians are often blessed *while* tithing but this is not necessarily *because* we're tithing. The Lord promises that "those who honour Me, I will honour" (1 Sam 2:30) so we can expect God to bless us, not because of our good work in tithing, but for our motive in honouring Him.

Conversely, if we believe we should tithe and then don't, we can expect our conscience to bother us. This is now not the tithing issue at all, but rather sinning against conscience. Paul talks about this in relation to eating meat sacrificed to idols:

> 22. The faith which you have, have as your own conviction before God. Happy is he who does not condemn himself in what he approves.
> 23. But he who doubts is condemned if he eats, because his eating is not from faith, and *whatever is not from faith is sin* (Rom 14:22-23, emphasis added)

So those who have been tithing because they felt conscience-stricken if they didn't, need to be convinced that they don't have to before they can stop in faith. Otherwise they will sin against their consciences and walk in condemnation.

10. Summary

To summarise the arguments made in this study:

There is much disagreement and no authoritative teaching on tithing outside the Scriptures. The most accurate is *Encyclopaedia Judaica*'s summation that there were two distinct uses for the one tithe.

The Law of Moses proclaims a very different system of tithing from what is generally understood today. The primary use of the tithe was to provide holiday fare for the Israelites after harvest; its secondary purpose was to provide income for the Levites and some extra for the poor.

In that Law is a revelation of the goodness of God which we can still enjoy today, and thereby receive greater motivation to serve Him with our whole hearts, knowing that He cares about everything we need, even holidays.

Our present-day civil law requires employers to pay all employees for five or six weeks holidays every year, thereby handing over approximately a tithe for that time, and we can enjoy this provision as being from God and for our welfare. If we are self-employed, we can give ourselves the same.

We must still be careful to maintain the distinction between the Old and New Covenants when considering the will of God for today. For Christians there is no law of tithing, no compulsory holiday, no mandatory requirement to give away one tenth, or three tenths, or even one thirtieth, of all income.

Jesus does require all disciples to give over to His ownership every possession and for every disciple to consciously acknowledge that they are now, and will remain, only stewards of whatever He leaves under their control. This means that any giving that is done in response to fear or legalism, rather than in response to His command to each of us, is actually disobedience.

The New Testament gives guidelines for giving which are like the secondary use of the Old Testament tithe, i.e. to provide an income for those who have no means of gaining one. In those days these were the ministers and the poor. The ministers, i.e. those in "full-time ministry", were the New Testament equivalent of the Old Testament's Levites. The poor were defined as the widows, the orphans, the handicapped, and the strangers. Their needs were not to be satisfied by purely material help but also by friendship and hospitality.

In giving to our ministers today, we should seek to provide an income for them rather than to fund corporate schemes that may not be the will of God. We need to accept more personal responsibility, since the things left by Jesus in our individual stewardship are not meant to be handed over to someone else to administer. Our failures in this area have largely contributed to the waste of our resources.

As for the poor today in New Zealand, our giving must take account of our changing society, in case help from general taxation fails. Financial restructuring of our Welfare State can quickly disadvantage the vulnerable among us so we need to constantly monitor the situation. As well as people's financial needs, we are called to address their emotional and spiritual needs by individually reaching out in hospitality.

To give to those who have nothing at all, I believe we should give outside of New Zealand, to wherever there is no Welfare State and, ideally, where Christian groups like International Needs have been specifically set up to facilitate this in His name.

It is essential in all these things that we remember and facilitate the intention of God, which is not only to redistribute wealth and meet genuine needs around us, but also to accomplish a work within us. That is, to bring forth in each of us the character of God Himself, the love that is generous and causes us to give freely.

11. How Then Should We Live and Give?

Karoshi, Death by Overwork

I first became aware of death by overwork in 1989 through a *Time* magazine article, "Coming to Grips With *Karoshi* (the Japanese try to set limits on their stressful work ethic)".[38] It began:

> Kiyoto Muramatsu was surprised when her husband Fumio, 41, told her one day last June that he would be home later that evening. It was rare for the busy metal-shutter salesman from Fukuroi, a small city southwest of Tokyo, to return on a weeknight rather than lodge near his office, several hours' driving time away. That evening, before falling asleep, he complained of feeling ill but assured his wife that "I just need to get some rest." In the early-morning hours, he died of a stroke. Muramatsu's widow now claims that long work hours and stressful responsibilities killed her husband.
>
> The diligence of employees like Muramatsu has been widely praised as the backbone of Japan's economic success. Slowly, however, even the hardworking Japanese are coming to question their indefatigable work habits, as they realize that stress and fatigue from long hours on the job can be a cause of ill health, including heart attacks and strokes. Each year about 500 families of kigyo senshi, or corporate soldiers, who have died of what appear to be stress-related ailments apply for workmen's compensation; about 10% are awarded such grants. Death from overwork even has a name: *karoshi*…

---

38 *Time,* Jan 30, 1989, p. 51

The United Nations has also recognised the phenomenon, accepting the Japanese name. Their International Labour Organisation (ILO) reports:

> Here are some typical cases of *Karoshi*:
> • Mr A worked at a major snack food processing company for as long as 110 hours a week (not a month) and died from heart attack at the age of 34. His death was approved as work-related by the Labour Standards Office.
> • Mr B, a bus driver, whose death was also approved as work-related, worked more than 3,000 hours a year. He did not have a day off in the 15 days before he had stroke at the age of 37.
> • Mr C worked in a large printing company in Tokyo for 4,320 hours a year including night work and died from stroke at the age of 58. His widow received a workers' compensation 14 years after her husband's death.
> • Ms D, a 22 year-old nurse, died from a heart attack after 34 hours' continuous duty five times a month.[39]

I had never heard of this before because here in New Zealand, we have a fairly relaxed lifestyle. I had taken our working conditions for granted, not knowing that we were the first nation in the world to introduce the 8 hour day, 40 hour week in 1840, thanks to Samuel Parnell.[40]

Time explained that in 1989, Japanese workers were working the longest hours of any of the major industrialised countries:

> On average, they spend as much as 500 more hours a year on the job than do their counterparts in West Germany and France, 200 more than those in the U.S. and Britain. Only 1 out of 3 workers enjoys a five-day workweek. Employees by and large use just half their paid vacation time, generally 15 days a year. "They worry that if they take time off, there will be too much work when they return, or it will cause trouble to their co-workers," says Osamu

---

39 www.ilo.org/safework/info/publications/WCMS_211571/lang--en/index.htm, 1 May, 2015.
40 www.jobsletter.org.nz/jbl19510.htm, 13 May, 2015.

Naito of the leisure-development section at the Ministry of International Trade and Industry (MITI).

Japanese corporate culture also has murky lines between work and leisure:

Says Toshio Kameda of the Labor Ministry's compensation division: "How do you categorize taking subordinates drinking after work, playing golf with clients on weekends and enduring a long commute?"

They therefore set up a leisure-development section within government, aiming to reduce work time from the average of 261 work days per year to 223 days within three years; public offices began closing two Saturdays a month.

To reduce the seemingly endless sense of responsibility workers apply to their jobs, MITI plans a series of leisure-promotion campaigns. Among other things, the ministry is sending a delegation to Brazil and Mexico to study government and community support of leisure activities. As part of its work, the group intends to observe the nature of community support for Brazil's Santos football team and for Mexican mariachi performances. Four couples will also be dispatched in February to Barcelona, Paris, Los Angeles and Vancouver to gain first-hand experience on how the locals enjoy themselves.[41]

The Japanese have been finding out the hard way what we in the West too often take for granted or completely fail to recognise - the extraordinary benefit of our Judaeo-Christian heritage.

'No-Vacation Nation'?

It's not just the Japanese. Now the U.S.A. is finding out the hard way. *Time* magazine have been looking closer to home, and in June 2015 published an article headlined, "Saving the Vacation – what must be done to revive a cherished American

---

41 *Time*, 30 Jan 1989, p.53

Graeme Carlé

institution":

> Ninety-six percent of American workers recognize the importance of taking vacation... Elementary research suggests it's restorative and good for heart health. But over the last 30 years, the U.S. has become a no-vacation nation, as the... Center for Economic and Policy Research once called it.[42]

They have seven national holidays annually but paid vacations are an employer's choice:

> The U.S. is the only advanced economy that does not require employers to offer paid holidays or time off. This bears repeating: it's the only developed economy that promises no paid vacation. *Zilch.* The U.S.'s few companions in time-off stinginess include Kiribati, the Federated States of Micronesia and the Kingdom of Tonga. Not even a single U.S. state has a paid-vacation law on the books.[43]

Disney's latest contract, which *Time* says is better than most, gives workers in the Magic Kingdom 10 days annual leave for the first four years of employment, 15 days from the fifth. *Time* noted that in 2013, the average American worker with access to vacations took 23 days, including the seven statutory holidays, compared to 27.3 between 1976 and 2000, concluding:

> Despite steady gains in productivity, the American worker has, in little more than a decade, ceded a full week of vacation to the employer, with no wage growth to show for it.

Why?

> Take a week off? Maybe your job won't be there when you come back... 17% of surveyed managers suggested that the employees who took all their earned days were less dedicated, and 13% considered those employees less likely

---

42 *Time*, 1 June 2015, p.34
43 *ibid*, p.35 Emphasis in original.

to get promoted in the future.

The outcome?

> By 2001, a third of Americans said they were chronically overworked, according to a Families and Work Institute study. Exhausting days lead to lethargic, stress-filled (and accordingly sleepless) nights. The body and mind take big hits; studies link overwork to depression and cardiovascular problems.[44]

It is surely no accident that this affliction is striking the nation whose churches have most taught tithing as a church tax instead of, as the Law of Moses taught, a holiday pay.

To find out more, see the Center for Occupational & Environmental Health at the University of California, Irvine.[45]

Personal Testimony

In my own case, for many years God kept me considering the use of the tithe for the annual holiday. I had almost burnt-out and, feeling like I had nothing left to give, I was desperately looking for a spiritual reason, such as a demonic attack. The Lord's answer to me was embarrassing but liberating as He spoke to me in the midst of this study. Up until then, while I had seen what was wrong in the teaching of tithing as a tax on Christians, I hadn't yet seen *why* God had established the tithe in Israel and the value of proper holidays. I had not actually applied its lessons to my own situation and that was my problem!

In response to His gentle reproof, I brought forward some annual leave to spend three whole weeks with my family, setting out to enjoy it in His presence and to indulge the legitimate desires of our hearts. We did the things for which we didn't

---

44 *ibid*, p.36
45 www.coeh.uci.edu/faculty/coeh_fac/dr_schnall.htm, accessed 6 May, 2015.

usually have time, lying about in the sun, reading novels, and watching movies we'd missed. We celebrated the joy of living with our children, swimming and sand-castling at the beach, visiting the zoo, playing on the swings at the park. By the end of the holiday, having done all these things with the Lord and feeling so much closer to my family, I was completely restored, wanting to serve Him more and to give more.

I came to rejoice again in His goodness, for the provision of times of rest, recreation and refreshment. It's my whole-hearted hope that this study may produce similar fruit in the reader.

Holidays In General

In order to compare the use of the tithe in Israel with our present-day holidays, I sought to establish what exactly is relaxing and what length of time is needed.

So, what is relaxing, and why?

Firstly, what were ancient Israel's issues and needs? They were primarily an agrarian society. With their largest cities small by today's standards, they were spread throughout the whole land with no means of rapid communication like today's phones, texts, or e-mail, or mass communication such as newspapers, radio, or television. Accordingly, one of their basic problems was rural isolation: they needed to gather together as a nation, and they did this three times a year (Ex 23:14).

Their gatherings had three major benefits:

(i) Every Israelite family was able to hear first-hand the word of God through the current leaders He had appointed:

> "Then Moses summoned all Israel, and said to them, 'Hear O Israel... that you may learn...'" (Deut 5:1)

> "The word that came to Jeremiah from the LORD, saying, 'Stand in the gate of the LORD's house and proclaim there this word and say, "Hear the word of the LORD, all you of Judah, who enter by these gates to worship the LORD!" ' " (Jer 7:1-2)

"And they made a proclamation to all the exiles that they should assemble at Jerusalem... Then Ezra the priest stood up and said to them..." (Ezra 10:7-10).

(ii) It helped them remember their unique calling as a *nation* (Deut 4:10).

(iii) It was a truly grand social occasion. As well as being important spiritually and nationally, their feasts were enjoyable, relaxing, and not too frequent, so it was worth putting in the effort of travelling to Jerusalem.

In stark contrast, our need for relaxation today may be best satisfied by the completely opposite behaviour, i.e. by avoiding society rather than by seeking it. Many of us are in danger of being completely overwhelmed by our communications, much of it trivial, and our social relationships. Internet connections, books, newspapers, magazines, newsletters, videos, movies, radio, and television keep us in constant and, at times, overly intrusive contact with what is happening in both the world and the Body of Christ. Our gathering together is never a problem in terms of opportunity or distance, whether for Sunday or mid-week meetings, house-groups, church camps or conferences, and our relationships can be maintained so easily, with an ever-increasing number of people, not only by daily contact, for most of us are city dwellers, but also by telephone, texts, answer-phone, mail, and social media.

We may therefore need to take time away from everyone and everything. However, we are all different so we each need to find what we most need before God.

We also don't need to go to Jerusalem to hear from Him because the Holy Spirit speaks to everyone who has ears to hear, both in our private devotions and in our meetings. On the other hand, many of us may find it deeply refreshing to go to a Christian conference, whether in a busy city or quiet countryside.

As for how long we should be on holiday, it is hard to get an exact correlation between Israel then and us today. Israel worked a six day week, in contrast to our usual five, and they had a very strict Sabbath rest on the seventh day (Lev 23:1-3), as well as every seventh and fiftieth year (Lev 25:1-22), even if they didn't always adhere to these (2 Chron 36:21). What we can say is that Israel had to cease all work quite frequently. It is my estimation that in addition to their weekly rest, and depending on their location, in order to keep the festal Sabbaths, new moons and Feast of Tabernacles, the Israelites were every year to cease working on between twenty and thirty days (see Appendix C). That is roughly three and a half to four and a half weeks spread out over the year, although once a year, during the Feast of Tabernacles, they had eight consecutive days.

In New Zealand today, our government requires all employers to pay all employees a minimum of four weeks annual leave plus two weeks of statutory holidays, scattered throughout the year. They also require at least two of the four weeks annual leave to be consecutive if desired by the employee.[46]

My Conclusions re Holidays

(i) Run and hide!
What would have been relaxing, refreshing, and stimulating for Israel then, because it was so different from their daily life, is for many of us today stressful, tiring, and tedious because for us it is simply more of the same of our daily life with no relief in sight.

Accordingly, while God is for holidays in general, our application must be individual and personal. While some may

---

46 www.dol.govt.nz/er/holidaysandleave/annualleave/, 10 Apr 2015.

enjoy getting together on holidays, what I personally need at holiday time is *not* to meet with more people but rather to temporarily become a hermit!

This is especially true when everything's going wonderfully well in ministry:

> 30. The apostles gathered together with Jesus; and they reported to Him all that they had done and taught.
> 31. And He said to them, "Come away by yourselves to a secluded place and rest a while" (for there were many people coming and going, and they did not even have time to eat).
> 32. They went away in the boat to a secluded place by themselves (Mark 6:30-32)

Those in ministry or missionaries can often feel this is too self-indulgent; those who are self-employed may feel they can't afford to - the truth is, we can't afford *not* to. When renovating our family home, I really had to get away to stop the unfinished repairs playing on my mind. It also helps to be removed from our usual vantage point so we can get a fresh perspective.

(ii) Three consecutive weeks

As well as the Scriptures, I love the findings of an IBM staff report[47] which was commissioned to investigate why some of their young executives were 'burning out' while their older men were coping well with the same level of stress. The primary reason, it found, was because the older men had well-developed leisure habits, which gave them better recuperative powers than the younger men who had simply kept working, not taking their annual leave because they had been too busy.

The report recommended not only that all staff should develop and improve their personal leisure habits but also

---

47 Unfortunately, I am unable to give a reference because I have not been able to track it down, only hearing about it in the early 1980s from a friend in IBM NZ management.

mandated holidays, adding that these should be at least three weeks in duration. Their reasoning:

(a) The first week addresses fatigue and the past. It allows our minds to unwind and our bodies to catch up on lost sleep and recuperate from fatigue, restocking our normal reservoir of energy.

(b) The second week is for enjoying the present. With our minds relaxed and our energy restored, it is for play rather than work. At the end of the second week, however, many make the mistake of thinking that's enough - they feel rested, they've had some recreation, so they return to work without taking the third week. But third week is just as important as the first two:

(c) The third week is for planning and the future. We all need time to consider what lies ahead but ideally after rest and recreation so that we are at our best. It's hard to objectively plan future work when you're exhausted.

When I heard this, it made such good sense to me that for many years now I have taken three consecutive weeks of holiday instead of throughout the whole year. I have found it really helpful to watch myself quite naturally go through these three stages of resting from the past, enjoying the present, and planning for the future.

My conclusion then is that like Israel of two to four thousand years ago, we too need three to five weeks holidays per year to be doing something, almost anything, different from our normal lives. The IBM report accurately identified a problem of our times and a sound solution.

(iii) Mandated even by secular government

I find it very gratifying that the principles of holidays revealed to Moses some 3,500 years ago are still being practised in our society today, even if we haven't recognised it. Isn't ironic that our avowedly secular government is being more faithful to the Scriptural practice of tithing than our churches who have too often turned it into an oppressive tax on the poor? God has preserved holidays for us, despite our bad teaching.

Personal Giving

Without "letting the left hand know what the right hand is doing" by giving details, here's how I believe God has led me to give over the last forty years.

In response to what I believed the Lord was saying to me, when I was converted in 1973 I dropped out of studying electronics engineering and, after only a year and a half of preparation, went into full-time ministry, travelling with Marcus Ardern, a widely-known and respected preacher and teacher. For the next seven years of speaking on campuses, city streets, in churches, and at camps, I lived like Marcus "by faith", reliant on God and His people for all my needs, and trying to put into practice what Jesus had told those He had called to this work. I experienced first-hand the answer Jesus gave Peter:

> 28. Peter began to say to Him, "Behold, we have left everything and followed You."
> 29. Jesus said, "Truly I say to you, there is no one who has left house or brothers or sisters or mother or father or children or farms, for My sake and for the gospel's sake,
> 30. but that he shall receive a hundred times as much now in the present age, houses and brothers and sisters and mothers and children and farms, along with persecutions; and in the world to come, eternal life"
> (Mark 10:28-30)

I know just how Peter felt, having left everything, then later wondering if I'd done the right thing, but I found that I had indeed hundreds of new brothers and sisters and mothers and children and places where I was welcome to stay, as well as a constant provision. Financially, this was less than a fifth of what I had earned in previous work but I never lacked and I loved the life.

Then in 1982, I married. My wife had also worked in full-time ministry for several years with YWAM (Youth With A Mission) so she too knew the "by faith" life-style. She was now a student and I felt the Lord was saying I should follow Deuteronomy 24:5:

> When a man takes a new wife, he shall not go out with the army nor be charged with any duty; he shall be free at home one year and shall give happiness to his wife whom he has taken.

Accordingly, I re-joined the secular work-force as a lowly clerk, where my income immediately doubled, my work hours dropped to 40 hours a week, every night and weekend was free, and I received annual leave and frequent statutory holidays!

However, I also found myself in my thirties where many of my contemporaries had been in their twenties: with a wife, a house, a mortgage and soon after, three small children. Our giving changed dramatically. When I say a mortgage, it was actually two, plus four small private low interest and interest-free loans from family and friends, to buy a house that God was clearly calling us to buy. Most of our "giving" then became to repay these private loans and one of the mortgages because we didn't feel free to give away what wasn't really ours.

We also had an open home for hospitality with many Christian workers passing through. We co-founded a church which also out-worked these teachings for the next fifteen years. As we prospered, we became able to give freely and spontaneously as well as by setting up monthly automatic payments to our home church, World Vision and mission work, just as we felt the Lord was leading us.

In 1985, an opportunity arose for me to halve my secular work so I set up The Work Charitable Trust, enabling me to work half-time as an interdenominational Bible teacher while Christian friends supported me financially. I saw this as my 'tent-making', imitating Paul (Acts 18:3-5).

In 1997, I returned to a full-time 'faith' ministry, serving briefly in Nepal with INF (International Nepali Fellowship) and for a year in Colorado with YWAM (Youth With A Mission). In 2002, I became a Baptist minister where for the first time, and for seven years, I received a standard income.

In all of this, in every circumstance, we were constantly striving to be obedient to Jesus in all our giving.

Today, I am again working as an itinerant Bible teacher and writer, trusting in God and His people for my income, as the ancient Levites did.

Giving in general

> Watch over your heart with all diligence,
> For from it flow the springs of life (Prov 4:23)

We must therefore diligently watch our hearts for any sign of the love of money rather than God. However, giving also provides every one of us with wonderful opportunities to grow spiritually, increasing our intimate relationship with Him through learning to hear His voice more clearly and walking in His Spirit. Jesus promised that as we put into practice Matthew 6:1-18, i.e. the spiritual disciplines of giving in secret, praying in secret and fasting in secret, the reward from our Father who sees in secret will be an increasing spirituality and sensitivity, and isn't that our goal?

Sometimes, however, our giving can inspire others to do similarly:

> "Let your light shine before men in such a way that they may see your good works, and glorify your Father who is in heaven" (Matt 5:16)

As a new Christian, I was greatly inspired by the love and generosity of one of my new sisters, Diana. She was a nurse and unmarried but very aware of the pressures faced by mothers with small children, both financially and emotionally, so she decided to bless them. Each week, she would choose a young mother, arrange for child-care, take her out for lunch and then take her shopping for whatever she wanted, whether some pampering in a beauty parlour or some new clothes.

Whenever we perceive a need, our first response should be to be loving and generous but subject to the leading of the Holy Spirit. Some needs, whether of an individual or of church organisations, may be due to people being outside of the will of God. To give in such circumstances may actually encourage their carelessness or rebellion.

In general, however, we should be generous where the New Testament directs, to support the poor and to support ministers, whether full-time or part-time, which exactly parallels the Old Testament support of the poor and the Levites.

The Poor

As mentioned earlier, we should watch developments in our nation, continually reassessing who are our poor and what their needs are. One area that I see that will become increasingly critical in New Zealand is the care of our elderly. Often cut off from earning by their age, they are increasingly isolated by modern social structures from the younger members of their families who, Biblically, should be their primary support.

The Levites

The Levites were more than just the rest of the tribe of the priests. They were: the worship leaders, musicians and singers; the administrators of the temple, being the treasurers and gate-keepers (1 Chron 23:3-5, 24-32, 25:6-7, 26:19-20); the civil administrators and judges of the nation (1 Chron 26:29-32); the guardians of "all measures of volume and size" (1 Chron 23:29).

Their equivalent today therefore is seen not only in preachers, teachers, and church administrators, but also in worship leaders and Christian artists of all kinds, whom we partially support by buying their work or paying to go to their concerts. Today's Levites are also Christian youth workers, community, and social workers (e.g. in the Open Homes Foundation,[48] Christians Against Poverty,[49] etc.) and the staff of various overseas aid agencies (such as International Needs,[50] Interserve,[51] Servants,[52] TEAR Fund,[53] and World Vision[54]). Giving to support these is equivalent to giving to support the Levites and the Holy Spirit is already directing many believers in this way. Hopefully, this study provides further Biblical confirmation for doing so.

I realise this may not be popular with those who believe in dividing the Body of Christ into church and "para-church", but this concept is unhelpful. We must learn to think in terms of the Kingdom of God, and the activity of our King, whether in our meetings or in our world; either way, it is Biblical to actively support and finance these full-time or part-time workers. In doing so, we will be co-workers with the truth, participating in the harvest of souls, as John wrote:

> 5. Beloved, you are acting faithfully in whatever you accomplish for the brethren, and especially when they are strangers;
> 6. ... You will do well to send them om their way in a manner worthy of God.

---

48 Open Home Foundation (NZ), www.ohf.org.nz
49 Christians Against Poverty (NZ), www.capnz.org
50 International Needs (NZ), www.internationalneeds.org.nz
51 Interserve (NZ), www.interserve.org.nz
52 Servants to Asia's Urban Poor, http://servantsasia.org
53 TEARFund (NZ), www.tearfund.org.nz
54 World Vision (NZ), www.worldvision.org.nz

7. For they went out for the sake of the Name, accepting nothing more from the Gentiles.
8. Therefore we ought to suport such men, so that we may be fellow workers with the truth (3 John1:5-8)

Our Experiments with Truth[55]

In 1982, the Baptist church I was attending was infected with the Shepherding and Discipleship teaching and quickly self-destructed. From being a thriving charismatic gathering of hundreds led by a wonderful and loving minister with seven elders with twelve home-groups, the flock was scattered in every direction - the minister became domineering, drove out five of the elders and eleven of the home-group leaders, before being "promoted" and sent out as an "apostle". I and our home-group were deregistered for disagreeing with the teaching and being "disloyal" to the "father of the house". The one remaining home group leader then became the new minister and the flock continued to scatter.

Many of those hurt and disillusioned by this foolish teaching began to re-gather at our home-group which grew from six to sixty and then became three co-operating home-groups. With no Sunday church now, we eventually began fortnightly Sunday morning meetings in two school halls.

Among our leading couples were several new to town from similar church and ministry splits so we set out to create a new style of church, based on each person hearing and following Jesus (John 10:3-5, 27). As we saw it, it's better to light a small candle than to curse the darkness.

We found our new friends came from Baptist, Apostolic, Brethren, Roman Catholic, Presbyterian, Assembly of God, Dutch Reform, Salvation Army, Agape Force and YWAM backgrounds. Aiming to learn from the strengths and

---

55 I have always liked the subtitle of Gandhi's autobiography, *The Story of My Experiments with Truth*, New York; Penguin Books, 1983.

weaknesses of all of our past experiences, we resolved that we would let go all church dogma and unashamedly experiment with, firstly, whatever the Scripture taught regarding everything (2 Tim 3:16-17) and, secondly, whatever "seemed good to the Holy Spirit and to us" (Acts 15:28). Accordingly, we majored on worshipping God and growing in Him, studying the Bible, everyone contributing in our meetings, showing hospitality and "equipping the saints" to work for God wherever they were (Acts 2:42, Eph 4:12).

When it came to finances, we had all seen or heard of the problems caused by rich churches with gold-plated altars in impoverished communities, as well as the in-fighting caused by church structure – the deacons vs. the pastor/minister vs. the elders vs. the congregation – as they all tried to decide what to do with everyone else's money. Accordingly, we decided to experiment with having no building, no "blind" collections and therefore no central pool of funds other than for rent. For the next fifteen years the results were, I believe, outstanding.

(i) No building

We rented our local school assembly hall for $1 a week per adult and they gave us several class-rooms for our children's Sunday school, the staff-room for our crèche and Sunday lunches, an adventure play-ground, a swimming pool, a soccer field and off-street parking. No other church in town had such great facilities, and all for one dollar a week each.

The downsides were that we had to set-up the hall and classrooms every week (the Sunday school, for example, was not able to create an appropriate warm, creative environment) and bring our own sound-system (our musicians' own) but they allowed us to store some gear at the school.

However, we felt we were achieving the Scriptures' descriptions of how the Early Church worked:

(a) Effective use of existing public premises when unused.

After the Day of Pentecost, we see the Early Church had no church buildings, meeting instead from house to house (Acts 2:46) and for larger gatherings, in public areas of the Temple (Acts 5:12). Paul planted many churches without any buildings other than homes (Acts 16:15, 17:5-9, 18:4-7), the marketplace (Acts 17:22) and "the school of Tyrannus" (Acts 19:9). It is usually assumed that the latter was a lecture hall, probably attached to a gymnasia as found in every Greek city, and unused during the heat of the day.[56]

(b) We had no need for mortgages, rates, insurance, and building maintenance costs. Our taxes already pay for our schools and the premises were unused on weekends. It was a win-win outcome because the school received extra funding, our frequent presence deterred vandalism and we gave gifts to the staffroom including home cooking and, what was new technology then, a microwave and a water-cooler.

(ii) No "blind" collections

Most churches take up a collection in every service which creates a pool of funds to be administered, which is where strife often begins. We instead placed a treasury box by the entrance, as in Mark 12:41-44, but with six labelled slots so that everyone giving had to decide where to give. No collections

---

56 The Western text adds, 'from the fifth hour to the tenth,' meaning 11 a.m. until 4 p.m. 'If so, Paul took advantage of the hottest hours of the day when most people rested after the midday meal. The hall would normally be vacant, and perhaps rent cheaper, after Tyrannus, or whoever the teacher was, lectured in the cooler morning hours (see Martial 9:68; 12:57; Juvenal 7:222-226). This would allow Paul to work at his own trade during business hours (Acts 20:34; 1 Cor 4:12). Then, instead of resting, he engaged in mission work and apologetics when those in trades and business were at leisure to hear him. As a result, "all the residents of Asia heard the word of the Lord, both Jews and Greeks" (Acts 19:10).' www.biblicaltraining.org/library/tyrannus#sthash.BGOPtAoA.dpuf, 23 Jun, 2015.

were "blind"; all were targeted to specific issues.

One slot, for example, was for the visiting speaker. Rather than have a committee decide how much they should receive, we encouraged every hearer to respond as individuals to what they personally had received (Gal 6:6-8). It seemed to us that the churches in Macedonia (2 Cor 11:9) or Philippi (Phil 4:15-16) didn't have a leader or church committee deciding the amount Paul should receive.

Of course, many churches today take up special "love offerings" for visiting speakers which also avoids this problem; our slot simply facilitated that every week. This meant that some who spoke only once or twice might receive thousands of dollars because their on-going work or ministry was considered so valuable that we would "send them on their way in a manner worthy of God" (3 John 1:5-8).

Another slot was for our weekly rent and children's work, and three others were labelled for Christian workers amongst us, one being me (via The Work Trust, as mentioned earlier), another for Bruce, one of our worship leaders whom we were encouraging to minister in other places too, and the third for Ian and Jo, a wonderful couple who had become missionaries in Nepal.

These last three ministries were also supported by individuals using monthly automatic bank payments but we committed as a church to facilitate and ensure that all funds collected in this way would reach those nominated. This often simplified it for those sending small but frequent amounts overseas.

The last slot was for spontaneous issues that might arise at any time such as famine or disaster relief. On one memorable occasion, I was asked by a member if our church could help her financially by nominating her for this slot. She was already on a government benefit and I had been helping her for some time so I knew her troubles were due to her often misspending her benefit. Being also very aware of 1 Tim 5:3-10, I refused to promote her cause so she waited until I was away and asked another leader. He agreed but, to her horror, she only received $10.

When I returned, I went to see her and she complained to me about how miserly our church was and I was able to remind her that we encouraged everyone to give as led by God Himself. It seemed to me that just as He had led us to give thousands on other occasions, in her case He didn't want her to receive cash but to learn how to manage her finances properly.

(iii) No central pool of funds

We had heard, and seen in practice, that whoever controls the resources controls the group, so we avoided creating that control structure altogether. We instead left the money in the pockets of those to whom God had given it and encouraged them to decide for themselves how and where to give (2 Cor 9:7), to promote their own spiritual growth, as covered earlier in this study. Our over-riding principle was to encourage loving, cheerful generosity:

> 6. Now this I say, he who sows sparingly will also reap sparingly, and he who sows bountifully will also reap bountifully.
> 7. Each one must do just as he has purposed in his heart, not grudgingly or under compulsion, for God loves a cheerful giver![57]

---

57   2 Cor 9:6-7

Last Word for Pastors

Those of us who are ministers or leaders in churches need to regularly re-evaluate whether we are genuinely drawing the attention of our congregations to the needs as we see them in our work rather than to the needs *as God sees* them. Our calling and gifting is, after all, to equip the saints for their work of service for Him (Eph 4:12).

So how will we respond?

Without Fear

Over the years, I have spoken to many pastors about tithing. One very godly denominational leader responded that although he believed what we've studied here, he would not teach it because he was afraid his people would stop giving! As if God doesn't know the effects of His word?! Many others have expressed this fear, so let's remember God's requirement of us as ministers:

> ...the overseer must be above reproach as God's steward, not self-willed ...not fond of sordid gain (Tit 1:7)

Whose will are we seeking? Or is what we teach tainted by our fear or covetousness (2 Cor 9:5)?

With Perseverance

Several pastors have told me of apparent failures after they liberated their churches from tithing to experiment with hearing and obeying God Himself instead of just playing "follow the leader". They had suffered personally because some had indeed stopped giving to the church or the pastor's pet-project. To my delight, these leaders had responded by staying the distance, trusting that not only would the Scriptures be vindicated but also that the Holy Spirit in His people would correct any imbalance.

I too live in this attitude, paying the cost.

Accurately

Are we encouraging those most vulnerable to burn-out to take their necessary holidays? Everyone who does not have an employer ensuring they take due time off is vulnerable: all who are self-employed such as farmers, house-wives, solo parents, ministers, and missionaries. Are *we* taking our proper holidays?

> Be diligent to present yourself approved to God as a workman who does not need to be ashamed, *accurately* handling the word of truth (2 Tim 2:15, emphasis added)

If we are inaccurate in what we present as truth, we *will* be ashamed on that Day.

Encouraging spiritual growth

Giving is a primary means of godliness and overcoming Mammon, as we saw in "Four Kinds of Lovers". If we are teaching tithing wrongly, we are stunting our congregations' spirituality. We must therefore release, teach, and encourage our people to be led by the Spirit of God Himself in giving.

Faithfully building

I believe with all my heart those of us in ministry should lead from the front, not just in our meetings but in our daily lives regarding funding. This requires more Biblical faith *of us* than if we subject our people to our own taxation system. We also run the risk that some of our plans and programs may be revealed as our will rather than His but, after all, as Solomon says:

> Unless the Lord builds the house, they labour in vain who build it (Ps 127:1)

Let's build His way.

Appendix A – Extra-Biblical Jewish References

In the 3rd Century B.C., a light-hearted Jewish novella, *Tobit*, set in the 8th Century B.C., had the main character criticizing her kinsmen for their idolatry:

> 5. All my kinsmen, the whole house of Naphtali my ancestor, sacrificed on the mountains of Galilee to the calf which Jeroboam, king of Israel, had made in Dan;
>
> 6. at the festivals I was the only one to make the frequent journey Jerusalem prescribed for all Israel as an everlasting commandment. I used to hurry off to Jerusalem with the first-fruits of crops and herds, *the tithes* of the cattle, and the first shearings of the sheep;
>
> 7. and I gave them to *the priests* of Aaron's line for the altar, and *the tithe* of wine, corn, olive oil, pomegranates and other fruits *to the Levites* ministering in Jerusalem. The *second tithe* for the six years I converted into money, and I went and distributed it in Jerusalem year by year
>
> 8.[58] among *the orphans and widows*, and the [Gentile] *converts* who had attached themselves to Israel. Every *third year* when I brought it and gave it to them, we held a feast according to the rule laid down in the Law of Moses and the instructions given by Deborah, the mother of Hananiel our grandfather; for my father had died leaving me an orphan. (Tobit 1:5-8, emphasis added)[59]

---

[58] Some translations such as *The New Oxford Annotated Bible (New Revised Standard Version with the Apocrypha)* insert "A third tenth I would give to…" from other ancient authorities like Josephus. However, that would leave the second tithe undirected. See Maimonides next.

[59] *The New English Bible (with the Apocrypha)*, New York; Oxford University Press, 1971, p. 54 AP.

So Tobit's fictional great grandmother saw the Law as requiring their first-fruits offerings and tithes of the cattle for the priests (vss. 6-7) and two tithes of the harvested crops, one for the Levites (vs. 7) and the second for the needy (vs. 8). Also, "every third year", the tither was to partake of the feast with them (vs. 8).

Moses ben Maimon, also called Maimonides and the Rambam, was a 12th Century Halachic arbitrator and one of the most important figures in the history of Jewish scholarship. He calculated there were 613 commands in the Torah, 248 positive and 365 negative, i.e. prohibitive. He listed among the positives:

> 127. To separate a tithe of grain [and give it] to the Levites, as [Lev 27:30] states: "All the land's tithes...."
> 128. To separate the second tithe so that it can be eaten by its owners in Jerusalem, as [Deut 14:22] states: "You shall surely tithe...." According to the oral tradition, we learn that this refers to the second tithe.
> 129. For the Levites to separate a tenth from the tenth which they took from the Israelites and give it to the priests, as [Num 18:26] states: "Speak to the Levites..."
> 130. To separate the tithe for the poor instead of the second tithe in the third and sixth years of the seven-year [agricultural cycle], as [Deut 14:28] states: "At the end of three years, remove a tithe of all your crops...."[60]

He taught "according to the oral teaching", i.e. Jewish traditions, therefore, that the Levites received a tithe every year and the tither ate a second tithe every year but in the third and sixth years (from the Sabbatical year), the second tithe was given to the poor.

Today's *Encyclopaedia Judaica* (2007), however, sees the

---

60 www.chabad.org/library/article_cdo/aid/901703/jewish/Part-2.htm, 1 May, 2015. The Old Testament chapter and verse references are inserted because these didn't exist until Isaac Nathan ben Kalonymus created them in 1448 (chapters were invented in 1227 by Stephen Langton; New Testament verses by Robert Estienne in 1551).

Law as a collation of two separate codes, the Priestly and the Deuteronomic:

> Though the purpose of the tithe and its method of organization in the discussed period seem quite clear, serious problems from the religious-halakhic standpoint complicated the issue. From Ezra's time the whole pentateuchal literature was considered a total unity (the Law of Moses) and the people had to comply with the Torah as a whole. The various attitudes toward the tithe as reflected in the different sources and especially in the Priestly code, on the one hand, and the Deuteronomic code on the other, had to be combined and the contradictions to be harmonized. Thus for instance the two types of tithes prevalent at this period: "the first tithe" *(ma'aser ri'shan)* and "the second tithe" *(ma'aser sheni)* are the outcome of the contradiction between Num 18:21ff. and Deut 14:22ff. According to the priestly ordination, the tithe is to be given to the levite, whereas according to the Deuteronomic code, it is to be consumed by the owner at the central sanctuary. The rabbis, taking it for granted that both laws are of Mosaic origin and therefore equally binding, interpreted them as two different tributes: one to be given to the levite, "the first tithe"; and the other to be brought to Jerusalem and consumed there, "the second tithe." Theoretically, this was an excellent solution. However, from the practical point of view the implementation of these laws was almost impossible. The excise of 20% of the yield was too high, while a more serious problem was the destination of the tithe. There were very few levites in the Second Temple period – in contrast to the situation at the monarchical period – and so the tithe was automatically shifted to the priests. Because this does not comply with the Law, all kinds of explanations had to be provided in order to do away with this legal anomaly.[61]

---

61 *Encyclopaedia Judaica*, 2nd ed., Detroit; Keter Publishing House Ltd, 2007, Vol. 19. p. 739, emphasis added.

As can be seen in this study, I agree with the rabbis regarding the unity of the Torah but also resolve *Encyclopaedia Judaica*'s almost impossibly high excise of 20% by establishing that one tithe would have been enough for both purposes, due to the low number of Levites revealed in all the censuses, not just in the Second Temple period.

Appendix B – The Four Censuses of Israel

On leaving Egypt

When Israel first left Egypt, they were counted: the men of Israel, over the age of twenty and able to go to war but excluding the Levites, numbered 603,550 (Num 1:46-47, 2:32-33); the Levite males, from a month old and upward, numbered 22,000 (Num 3:39).

We see then that there were twenty seven times more men of Israel than there were Levite males. However, not only were these men to be warriors, they were also to be the bread-winners for their families so every male represented a family and their income. Accordingly, if the Levites were to receive the whole tithe every year, as we are often told today, every Levite male, down to one month old, would have received 2.7 times the average income of every other bread-winner in Israel. But one month old Levite baby boys would not need tithes because their Levite fathers would provide for their households.

Accordingly, if 10% of the Levite males were under twenty, the ratio of over twenty Levites to over twenty Israelite male would be 1:30, making their income exactly three times the average income. If 20% under twenty, the ratio becomes 1:34 and their income 3.4 times the average income.

In addition, although the priests were all Levites, they also had to be descendants of Aaron, Levi's great-grandson. The priests didn't receive tithes from the people, only the tithe of the other Levites who were not descendants of Aaron (Num 18:25-32); their primary provision was instead a portion of all the offerings of Israel, plus all first-fruit offerings (Num

18:8-20, Neh 10:34-37). So, although there were only a few priests initially, later there were many to be considered in ratio calculations, as we can see below.

It is clear that in the first census of Israel, the Levites were *at most* about one thirtieth of the nation.

Forty years later

Another census was taken after all the dealings in the wilderness including plagues, judgments and death from old age. There had been no tilling of the soil and no harvest to tithe there because Israel lived on manna so they were now about to begin tithing for the first time.

We find the men of Israel, over the age of twenty and excluding the Levites, numbered 601,730 (Num 26:51). The Levite males, from a month old and upward, numbered 23,000 (Num 26:62). This census gives us a ratio of 1:26 Levite to Israelite and the comments above apply again.

David's muster

In about 1000 B.C., the Levites numbered 38,000 (1 Chron 23:3) from a total of 1,300,000 fighting men (2 Sam 24:9), i.e. 1:33.

Returning from exile

The fourth census was taken when the nation was being restored to the land of Israel from Babylon. This time there was only the remnant: 25,406 men of Israel (Neh 7:7-38); 4,289 priests (Neh 7:39-42); and 752 Levites (Neh 7:43-60).

With the restoration to the land came the restoration of tithing and, remember, the priests did not receive the peoples' tithes - only the Levites' tithes but all first-fruits and portions of all the offerings - so they are left out of our calculations.

The ratio of Levites to Israelites therefore was 1:34.

In conclusion, these four censuses reveal a remarkable consistency in the number of Levites as a ratio of the number of Israelites, despite being taken at the most tumultuous times of Israel's history: they were only ever about one thirtieth of the nation's population. This means that if they had received the tithe every year, the Levites' income would have been three times the average income of everyone else. Only if they received the third-year tithe would it have been fair and equitable.

Appendix C – Israel's Holidays

The whole nation of Israel, except the priests, were strictly commanded to refrain from any work every Sabbath or seventh day (Matthew 12:5). The Jewish calendar was lunar, i.e. 29.53 days, so their year had at least 51 weeks but could be as many as 55 weeks:

> Months are either 29 or 30 days, corresponding to the 29½-day lunar cycle. Years are either 12 or 13 months, corresponding to the 12.4 month solar cycle… The problem with strictly lunar calendars is that there are approximately 12.4 lunar months in every solar year, so a 12-month lunar calendar is about 11 days shorter than a solar year and a 13-month lunar is about 19 longer than a solar year [i.e. the shortest year is 354 days and the longest 384 days].
>
> The months drift around the seasons on such a calendar: on a 12-month lunar calendar, the month of Nissan, which is supposed to occur in the Spring, would occur 11 days earlier in the season each year, eventually occurring in the Winter, the Fall, the Summer, and then the Spring again. On a 13-month lunar calendar, the same thing would happen in the other direction, and faster. To compensate for this drift, the Jewish calendar uses a 12-month lunar calendar with an extra month occasionally added. The month of Nissan occurs 11 days earlier each year for two or three years, and then jumps forward 30 days, balancing out the drift. In ancient times, this month was added by observation: the Sanhedrin observed the conditions of the weather, the crops and the livestock, and if these were not sufficiently advanced to be considered "spring," then the Sanhedrin inserted an additional month into the calendar to make sure that Pesach (Passover) would occur in the spring (it is, after all, referred to in the Torah as Chag he-Aviv, the Festival of Spring!)[62]

---

62 www.jewfaq.org/calendar.htm, 24 Apr, 2015. Comment in square brackets added.

They therefore rested on between 51 and 55 weekly Sabbaths every year.

Leviticus 23 tells us they were also to cease work on the first and seventh days of the Feast of Unleavened Bread (vss. 7-8), on the one-day Feast of Pentecost (vs. 21), on the one-day Feast of Trumpets (vss. 24-25), on the Day of Atonement (vss. 27-28) and on the first and eighth days of the Feast of Tabernacles (vss. 35 and 39). Later on, there were two more days to celebrate at Purim (Esth 9:16-28). The Feast of Dedication (John 10:22), today's Hanukkah, was celebrated for eight days but without Sabbaths. There were therefore nine holiday Sabbaths every year.

Then there were the twelve or thirteen "new moons". The new moon was synonymous with the first day of the month and celebrated under the Law (Num 10:10, 28:11-15). While not described there as a Sabbath, Amos quotes the unrighteous as complaining about not being able to trade on "the new moon" (Amos 8:5) and Ezekiel links "the day of the new moon" with the Sabbath as a non-working day (Ezek 46:1), making another twelve days of rest every year.

Some of these twenty-one festival Sabbaths of course coincided with weekly Sabbaths, creating "high Sabbaths", but this obviously varied year by year.

To all the Sabbaths, we need to add the week of Feast of Tabernacles which was celebrated in Jerusalem as mentioned earlier. While work was allowed during this week, it was still a holiday away from home. Also, time for travelling to Jerusalem which, for those from Galilee, would have added several days to both ends of the Festival.

Accordingly, we can say that in addition to their 51-55 strict weekly Sabbaths, and depending on their location, Israel was to cease working on another 25-30 days every year. With their six-day working week, this was four to five weeks holiday, almost a tenth of their year.

Other books by Graeme Carlé

Because of the Angels
(Unveiling 1 Corinthians 11:2-16)
This text has been largely lost to today's church because we have badly misunderstood some of Paul's Hebrew presuppositions regarding 'head', 'covering', the fall of Satan and spiritual warfare. Liberating for men and women of God as it restores much needed revelation on gender differences and relationships as well as the mystery of the Nazarite vow.

The Red Heifer's Ashes
(Mysteries of Ancient Israel)
Considered by Orthodox rabbis to be the greatest mystery of the Law of Moses, this is an astonishing revelation of Messiah. Every detail is gently unfolded as the reader today follows a supernatural path through the whole of the Old Testament, just as the two disciples did on the road to Emmaus.

Born of the Spirit
(A study guide for new believers)
This interactive Bible study is for all who want to develop their personal spirituality by checking the foundations of what Jude the Lord's youngest brother called 'the faith which was once for all delivered to the saints' (Jude 3). Avoiding all denominational allegiances, find out for yourself how God wants us to love, live and learn.

These books are available from
Emmaus Road Publishing
PO Box 38 823 Howick, Auckland 2014 New Zealand
www.emmausroad.org.nz

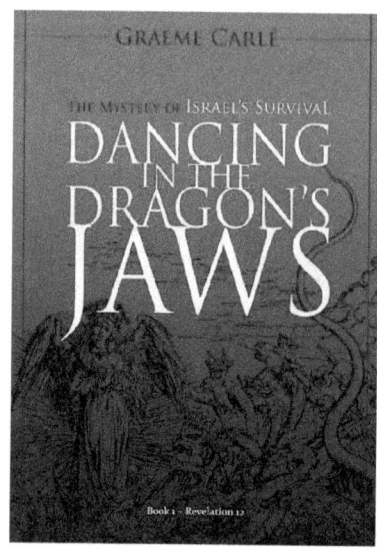

Book 1 in the Revelation series

Dancing in the Dragon's Jaws
The Mystery of Israel's Survival

Graeme Carlé

Why is the Book of Revelation so misunderstood? Wasn't its whole point to give revelation? Well, in typically Jewish manner, yes and no.

The Book of Revelation was written as an apocalypse, a Jewish literary genre which also includes the extraordinary Books of Daniel and Zechariah. Profound truths were concealed from outsiders and opponents using elaborate symbolism, to be understood only by those properly taught – as Jesus explains in Matthew 13:10-13.

The apostle John's original first century audience, having been led by Jewish Christians, would have readily understood his imagery from Jewish history. His plagues echo the ten plagues of Israel's exodus; his seven trumpets resonate of the Old Testament battle for Jericho.

Many think the keys to unlocking the Book of Revelation are lost. Not so. We still have Old Testament history and, for those who know where to look, full explanations of its symbols in the New Testament. What we need is the humility to learn from the first century Jewish believers the mysteries of the woman, the Messiah, the dragon, the comings of Elijah, and 'the times of the Gentiles'. From these we can understand God's continuing purpose for Israel.

Available from
Emmaus Road Publishing
PO Box 38 823 Howick, Auckland 2014 New Zealand
www.emmausroad.org.nz

ISBN 978-09582746-5-4

Book 2 in the Revelation series

Slouching Towards Bethlehem

The Rise of the Antichrists

Graeme Carlé

The Lost Keys of Revelation?
It is often thought today that the keys to understanding the Book of Revelation have been lost and are irretrievable – but they're not. They were just buried under centuries of rubble created by the Gentile church's foolish attempts to distance itself from its Jewish foundations. If, like any archaeologist, we dig carefully we can rediscover them.

In *Dancing in the Dragon's Jaws*, we found one key to understanding Revelation chapter 12 is the metaphorical "time, times and half a time" and we unlocked the last 4,000 years of Jewish history.

This book, *Slouching Towards Bethlehem*, unlocks Revelation chapter 13 and the last 2,000 years of the Christian era, with startling results. Not only can we now understand the forces shaping history and the deaths of some 270 million in 20th Century genocides but we can also project the future of Israel and the Middle East.

Available from
Emmaus Road Publishing
PO Box 38 823 Howick, Auckland 2014 New Zealand
www.emmausroad.org.nz

ISBN 978-0-9582746-8-5

Book 3 in the Revelation series

Gotta Serve Somebody
The Mystery of The Marks & 666

Graeme Carlé

Are you confused about 'The Mark of the Beast'?
You're not alone. The Mark and the number 666 have been controversial for centuries. Scholars and laymen alike have offered numerous interpretations, 'calculations' and wild guesses but most predictions have failed to materialize. Some say we just have to wait.

In this book, Graeme Carlé uses the keys recovered in the first two in his series (*Dancing in the Dragon's Jaws* and *Slouching Towards Bethlehem*) to unlock the symbols and 'times' of the most infamous and misunderstood mark in human history.

Instead of waiting for a world government or a global banking system that may never eventuate, Graeme believes and shows that The Mark is already here — and has been for the last 2,000 years! We've just not recognised it.

It is actually the beast's counterpart of marks that God Himself placed on the forehead and hand of His people at the Exodus and in the wilderness, with a numbering system of names as described in the Book of Numbers.

We don't need a profound theological education or esoteric enlightenment but we do need a basic grasp of Jewish history and the Old Testament, as understood by 1st Century Jewish believers in Jesus of Nazareth.

Available from
Emmaus Road Publishing
PO Box 38 823 Howick, Auckland 2014 New Zealand
www.emmausroad.org.nz

ISBN 978-0-9582746-9-2

www.ingramcontent.com/pod-product-compliance
Lightning Source LLC
Chambersburg PA
CBHW050436010526
44118CB00013B/1555